We all have interests to share.

Podcasts
and Screencasts

Podcasts
and Screencasts

TESOL Strategy Guide

DAVID KENT

Pedagogy Press

National Library of Australia Cataloguing-in-Publication entry:
Kent, David Bradley, author.
Podcasts and screencasts / David Kent.

ISBN: 9781925555097 (paperback) (3)
TESOL strategy guide ; 3.
Includes bibliographical references.
Teachers of English to Speakers of Other Languages.
Presentation graphics software.
Podcasts.
Educational technology.
Teaching—Aids and devices.
Communication and Technology—Study and teaching.
English language—Study and teaching—Foreign speakers.

Pedagogy Press. Sydney, Australia.
www.pedagogypress.com

First Edition.

For teachers everywhere.

CONTENTS

Preface

This *TESOL Strategy Guide,* number three in the set, arose out of the clear need to provide teacher training and a means of professional development to educators, living and working in the Republic of Korea. Many expatriate English language instructors have arrived in-country without training as a teacher or educator, and are often left to take care of their own professional development while engaged in teaching English to speakers of other languages (TESOL). As many of these teachers come to enjoy working as expatriates, they often begin to seek out their own professional development on topics that they wish to learn more about, on skills that they wish to gain, and on techniques that they wish to integrate within their classrooms. It is this need, which is common to all teachers of English in all contexts around the globe, that this book seeks to fill.

Organization of the text

Each *TESOL Strategy Guide* can be read standalone or in conjunction with others from the set. Each book provides information on a technology topic, and has been designed around a question-based format similar to the following:

- Overview
- What is … ?
- How can I use … ?
- What types of … exist?
- What elements are behind an effective … ?
- How can … lend itself to TESOL?
- How can I start using … with students?
- How do I evaluate a … ?
- What tools are available for … creation?
- How do I craft a … ?
- How would I use a tool to create a … ?
- What are the key points behind … use in the TESOL context?

A comprehensive list of resources with links to pertinent web sites and applications is included, along with lesson plan guides, example implementation techniques, and various free to use handouts for the teacher and student alike. A reference list of all works cited also allows those teachers with an interest in a particular topic to engage in reading further on the issues that most interest them and impact their learners.

It is hoped that this book will provide both education and something new for all teachers – be they trained or untrained, pre-service, in-service, seasoned, or retired.

1

Overview

Podcasts and screencasts are both disruptive innovations in that they started out using existing technology in ways that were different from intended practice (Christenson & Raynor, 2003), and they create a new market and value network that has since led to 'significant societal impact' (Assink, 2006). In the classroom, podcasts and screencasts can also be viewed as potentially disruptive by expanding the notion of audience from that of an audience of one (the teacher) or a few (classroom peers) to that of many (potentially the entire population of the globe). Further, by employing multimodal ways of knowing to expand the analytical and critical insights of learners (Hadjioannoou & Hutchinson, 2014), the use of podcasts and screencasts for learning holds the potential for the authentic use of content in ways that allow for the transmediation of knowledge that occurs in ways that are very different to those prior to the beginning of the 21st century, and in ways that allow students to become producers rather than consumers of knowledge-based media products.

Ultimately, this book focuses on the use and applicability of podcasts and screencasts in the context of teaching English to speakers of other languages (TESOL). The pedagogical possibilities arising from the use of these technological tools are provided, as is an overview of instructional strategies, tasks, and activities suitable for episode development with second-language learners of English. The steps involved in planning, producing, and publishing episodes are presented, along with tutorials, photocopiable handouts and templates, several evaluation techniques, and a comprehensive list of resources.

2

What are podcasts and screencasts?

In contrast to the mass produced broadcasting of content to a general audience, both podcasts and screencasts can be described as the narrowcasting of content, with authors providing specific knowledge, information, and insights to members. Narrowcasting in the classroom might see peers produce content for each other as well as interested stakeholders (like parents, the administration, and the teacher), which in turn allows them to become producers rather than consumers of media. In addition, as podcasts and screencasts not only allow users to selectively choose content, or subscribe to individual providers, this allows for the sustained exposure to specific content or knowledge over time, along with the ability to time- and place-shift access to this content, leading to anywhere, anytime listening or viewing – knowledge-on-demand.

Knowledge-on-demand (KOD), as Sampson, Karagiannidis, Schenone, and Cardinali (2002) see it, has emerged from the needs of a knowledge-based society that requires access to the anyone, anytime, anywhere delivery of education and training that is "adapted to the specific requirements and preferences of each individual citizen". Daily (2007) also suggests that, for technologies like podcasting and screencasting, there is the promotion of just-in-time (JIT) learning over just-in-case (JIC) learning. It is also likely that both access to content that individuals were specifically interested in, along with information that they needed 'right now', has led to the popularity and normalization of podcasting and screencasting with wider and wider audiences in a relatively short space of time.

Podcasting defined

The term *podcast* is one of several suggested by Hammersley (2004) for 'portable on demand' listening. Today, podcasting is usually recorded in the MP3 audio file format, but it can also be video-based (for example, appearing in the MP4 file format), and it can be played back on a variety of devices from smartphones to computers. Each new episode can be downloaded automatically (being either pushed or pulled) to a podcatcher (aggregators) capable of reading feed formats such as Really Simple Syndication (RSS), and are formats distinguishable from other digital audio or video formats like streaming media. Once the file has been listened to or watched, it can be automatically or manually deleted when another episode is to be released into the *podosphere* by the *podcaster* (the author or producer of a podcast). Normally, subscriptions to a podcast are free, and as such, there is essentially no cost for listening to or joining, and becoming a member of, a feed.

Terminology that has been used in association with podcasting and screencasting includes, among many more, terms such as: *vodcasting*, *vidcasting*, and *vlogging* for video podcasts; *blogcasting* for the podcasting of blog content; *Godcasting* for the podcasting of religious content; and, *learncasting* for the podcasting of educational content.

Screencasting defined

The term *screencast* was proposed by both McDonald and Cooley and chosen by Udell (2004) to represent the emerging genre. Screencasts capture what you do on any device with a screen (for example, a computer or an interactive whiteboard). Think of a screencast as a movie, where the stage is the display, the content the star, and you are the narrator. In many ways, screencasts can be thought of as video podcasts, and are mostly recorded, edited, and then published inside a web page or a blog post, or uploaded to a learning management system (LMS) like Moodle, Edmodo, or Schoology (as opposed to being distributed automatically by a feed). Screencasts are also often uploaded to public video sharing sites like YouTube where viewers might subscribe to the screencasters channel. Like podcasts, screencasts can humanize e-learning and enhance the educational experience of learners as they combine audio, text, and video, so that lessons can become more engaging and at the same time more accessible to a wider variety of learners – especially those that may need aural and visual explanation of content being presented to them simultaneously.

3

How can I use podcasts and screencasts?

Perhaps the best way to use podcasts and screencasts is in providing support for and supplementing direct instruction, which can take learning outside the classroom and also provides students with a means of creating their own learning content. Bell, Cockburn, Wingkvist, and Green (2007) have identified a number of positives and negatives associated with podcasting in educational contexts, some of which include access, flexibility and appeal. Simultaneously, these technologies can provide a fresh approach to engage students and improve the revision and instruction process while harnessing the promise of multimedia to enhance student learning (Mayer, 2003; Davis & McGrail, 2009; Liou & Peng, 2009).

Podcasts and screencasts provide flexibility as they allow students to listen to, or watch, an archive of course related content that is available anytime anywhere, and allows for flexible learning and convenience of access while being engaged in other activities or multitasking. This however, could mean that student attention is not focused on the learning material as environmental factors could impact upon concentration and the ability to hear content effectively, or occur in environments that may prevent note-taking (for example, public transport). Podcasts can also be appealing to those students who prefer auditory-based learning, and to those who do not like to read or may have problems with reading (for example, dyslexia). By the same token, screencasts might also appeal to those students who do not have reading problems but prefer aurally and visually oriented learning materials.

Podcasts and screencasts can also be useful for those learners who might have missed a lecture (if the class is recorded), as it can provide a first listening and note-taking session. The recording can also be used to gain access to a second listening by those who might need it (for example, second language learners). Such material can also be used in exam preparation as well as for reference purposes, and it allows students to review and study the content at their own pace, facilitating self-paced learning and perhaps also aspects of learner autonomy (Holec, 1987). Misuse might arise here though, as students might only use the podcasts and screencasts to review for exams or in cramming sessions rather than rely on other study methods.

Nevertheless, both podcasting and screencasting provide the opportunity to encourage active learning, and different types of learning, from visual (including videos, infographics, PDF content, and resource links) through to aural (listening clips). They can also involve students kinesthetically if the students themselves are engaged in the process of development of a podcast or screencast, and are involved in the preparation of any associated materials to use with it. The production process of both podcasts and screencasts is also well suited to providing for the development of multiple skills (for example, reading, writing, listening, and speaking) as well as of multiple literacies (including digital and media literacies).

4

What types of podcasts and screencasts exist?

Almost anything can be turned into a topic for a podcast or screencast, and as such, there is a great number of different podcasts and screencasts available, from the educational to the simply entertainment-based genre. Overall, however, there are only four main distinguishable types of podcast and four main distinguishable types of screencast, with different forms of content suited to one type or another.

Podcasts

Solo

Generally presented as a monolog, the solo podcast is one person talking on a particular topic where content can include news, opinions, or tutorials. It may be the easiest podcast to create as it involves only one person and a script. The challenge here is to retain audience interest with just one person speaking.

Interview

An interview format can be added to a solo podcast as a feature episode, or be established as the regular type of format from the very first episode. The challenge is to maintain a stream of interesting guests, as well as ensuring adequate recording quality (particularly if the interview is done over the phone or low-speed internet).

Multi-host

The multi-host type of podcast has more than one person talking or hosting the episode. This can allow for a more informal tone than a solo podcast, provide more than one viewpoint on a topic, spread the production effort, and allow for a show to continue if a presenter is absent. The challenge here may be the need to pay particular attention to scheduling as there are more people involved in planning and producing the podcast, and this could lead to higher editing needs.

Video

A *vodcast, vidcast,* or a *vlog,* is the same as a podcast but with video. It can provide an interesting and engaging format for a podcast, particularly one that is presented solo. However, challenges here are the editing needs from using video as well as audio, the need for higher-end production equipment, and ensuring a 'studio' that is quiet and free of audience distractions or annoyances (for example, those that might appear in the background).

Screencasts

Presentation

Presentation screencasts are usually lectures that are delivered while recording the presentation slides of a particular topic along with the narration of the speaker as voice-over. Challenges here can involve the editing out of pauses as well as issues concerning the updating of slides or other information at a later stage.

Demonstration

In this type of screencast, the screen is usually recorded to illustrate how to use a particular application or how to navigate a particular website. The screen is recorded with voice-over as narration. Challenges here are the need to keep talking and telling the user exactly where to look and what they need to do for each step. A script is essential, with editing to include annotations, captions, callouts, and zoom effects.

Streaming

A streaming screencast is played 'live', as it happens, but can be recorded simultaneously for later editing and archival purposes. Challenges here are ensuring that the bandwidth that is available to viewers allows for high resolution transmission of data, particularly if there is a reliance on visuals that the audience must interpret or be able to read. Further, the equipment being used must reliable, so that there is no break in the transmission, and powerful enough to record the screencast without any interference to the live stream.

Whiteboarding

The whiteboarding screencast captures the activity displayed on interactive whiteboards, from applications being used on various devices in a similar fashion, or from any blank canvas (such as a white slide in a presentation program) that is being used to simulate a whiteboard canvas. The challenge here is to write legibly so that the content is easily readable. Typically, the whiteboard is being recorded while the author provides a voice-over to accompany the visuals. The challenges here include ensuring that the handwriting is legible, and that the narration is audible. Also editing, depending on the application used to capture the activity, may not be possible, so attention to detail and correctness becomes imperative.

5

What elements are behind an effective podcast and screencast?

An effective podcast or screencast consists of several essential elements, and among the many points that can be discussed here, the more important involve preparation, structure, focus, highlighting of key points, editing, feedback, and scheduling. The effectiveness of each of these attributes will now be discussed for both podcasts and screencasts.

Podcasting
Preparation
Make notes before the show, and follow them. Do not attempt to improvise during the episode. Prepare questions for guests ahead of time, and provide these to guests prior to the episode recording. The notes and questions can then be used as the introduction, and as a reminder piece for show notes. Ensure that your hardware is of a good quality, and that it is functioning properly to avoid annoyances and problems during the recording.

Structure

Structure the podcast with a beginning, middle, and end, and use musical or sound collages to transition between topics. Title your podcast in a compelling way, and to reflect the content of the show. Keep the show length suitable to the audience: twenty to thirty minutes, up to an hour, or even as a little as five minutes.

Focus

Keep topics brief, and limit the coverage of each topic to between three to eight minutes.

Highlighting of key points

Use guests to vary the pace and tone of the episodes, but always bring them back on track if they go off topic. Get into a habit of repeating their key points for members for reinforcement. Remind members that you are documenting the key points, and that they will be included in show notes along with any resources mentioned regarding these points.

Editing

Delivery doesn't have to be perfect – use a human voice – but remove long pauses and significantly large errors from the episode. If something is funny laugh about it 'on air', but edit your laughter if it goes on for too long. Collate any resources or anything else that was mentioned to include in episode notes, and send a copy to the guest. (They may provide corrections or a few more 'nuggets' of information to include). Prepare the notes and the RSS feed and, when scheduled, release the episode and the accompanying show notes.

Feedback

Invite conversation by asking listeners to discuss the podcast. Take on board constructive feedback, and adapt your podcast accordingly. Ask for topics that listeners might want to hear about, initiate competitions, and involve members in the show.

Scheduling

Make it regular (for example, once a week). People who subscribe rely on you to release your podcasts on time! Episode 'air dates' need to be consistent, with a new episode released every week or every few weeks on a schedule that is both doable for you and familiar to subscribers. It is also important to update listeners if there will be a delay in the upload of a new episode. Perhaps prepare a podcast that can be used as a filler episode if something does happen to prevent your scheduled episode from being released on time.

Screencasting
Preparation
To create a script and notes that will guide the screencast, start with an outline and then perform a walkthrough before you begin recording. When recording, it would be a good idea to follow these notes and to make no attempt to improvise except to include a comment here and there, especially to mention a point that you think is important but forgot to include on the initial walkthrough. Ensure that your hardware is of good quality and is functioning well to avoid annoyances or problems during recording. For example, automatic updates are turned

off along with notifications to prevent them from popping up during recording.

Structure

Briefly introduce the topic, and provide a brief layout of the information to be covered (for example, how there are ten steps involved, and that there will be the use of two applications to achieve this). Have all of your 'screens' or areas to be recorded set up and sized appropriately, especially if you intend to move between applications or from one to another in a set sequence. You can use different applications, tabs in a browser, still images, or perhaps even a view of yourself over a webcam to create different screen areas. Ensure that the screen areas for capturing are all the same size, and break the screencast into sections by using these screen areas at the appropriate times.

Focus

If you need to go off topic or provide a detailed explanation for something, prepare an image that can be shown on screen. Alternatively, you could switch to record yourself on webcam, in which case you need to look presentable. This technique will get members familiar to either seeing you or the same image when more specific information is being covered. In either case, try to focus on audience needs. Also, pause as required, take a break so that you can remain focused, and stay on top of things while recording.

Highlighting of key points

Tell the viewer what they should be looking at, and use the mouse to highlight specific areas where viewers should be looking. Overlay annotations, captions, and callouts, and zoom into screen areas as necessary. Depending on the software being used, this can be done on the fly but it will likely have to be performed during the editing stage.

Editing

Remove comments that do not add anything to the screencast like, *"Oh, look. My alarm on the calendar just went off. Now let me see here. … Oh, okay. Right, then. Yes. … Let me go ahead and close that app then"*. (The app should have been closed prior to recording). If any comments like this are made, they should be edited out. Also, review your screencast for continuity issues, and ensure that your narration and video are synced. Record your video and narration at different times if necessary, or rely on software that records these as different tracks to make the editing process easier. When recording, be careful of exposing confidential data (like passwords). These will need to be removed during editing, or covered in post-production, if they do appear on screen. Add any overlays to add value to your cast (annotations, callouts, captions, zooms, and other effects like transitions or music).

Feedback

Invite comments – ask subscribers to provide feedback on the screencast, and to leave comments on your channel. Take on board constructive feedback from viewers (for example, if you are talking too quickly), and adapt your screencasting technique if necessary. Reply to comments if viewers ask for clarification of something presented on screen, or for further information about something that you have mentioned in the screencast. You may need to add an additional element to the screencast if there is a consistent issue among members. Ask for topics that subscribers want to see screencasted, and attempt to involve subscribers in the show (for example, by addressing comments online by selecting a few to highlight and a few to respond to at the end of the following screencast).

Scheduling

Casts need to be regular, released every few weeks or once a month, and on a timetable that becomes familiar to subscribers. In that way, viewers are likely to be eager to watch your next episode as soon as it is uploaded to your channel. The content that you choose to screencast will determine how long it will take to produce, and this will need to be considered when creating release schedules and 'air dates'. It is also important to update your channel members if there will be a delay in the upload of a screencast, and it may be a good idea to develop a screencast that can be used as a filler episode if something does happen to prevent your scheduled episode being released.

6

How can podcasting and screencasting lend themselves to TESOL?

Podcasting and screencasting can assist in the development of several language skills (such as speaking, listening, and pronunciation) during the production and narration stages of creation, as well as reading, writing and vocabulary development during the preparation stages. Students who participate in the production of podcasts and screencasts can also become familiar with the development of various forms of communication techniques (like, interview, speech, and presentation skills). Both formats will lead students to engage in listening skills practice, as well as seeing them concentrate on the need to speak effectively with attention to speed, pronunciation, and clarity of voice. Multiple literacies (from traditional literacy through to digital literacy and media literacy), along with other essential skills that include research skills, time management skills, and problem-solving skills, can also be developed through student podcast and screencast production and use.

Teachers too can also use podcasts and screencasts both directly and indirectly for teaching and learning. They can be used as supplementary content in a course to provide news and updates, answer student questions, and review content. More innovative uses include the provision of formative and more personalized feedback to students, and the reworking and resequencing of content (Ali, 2016).

A number of traditional TESOL classroom activities can be easily transferred to the podcast or screencast setting. These might include, but by no means limited to, activities involving commentaries, interviews, presentations, speeches, storytelling, retelling, and review. Additional activities can also include: developing a walking tour of a school or campus, recording a 'talk show', engaging in sportscasting, demonstrating the use of an application, or critiquing peer-developed podcasts and screencasts.

Teachers can use podcasts and screencasts to create targeted resources that are reusable, are used to resequence classroom or textbook content, and can be used both in and out of class for better use of the available time. An example is the development of language-point review podcasts, where students go over phrases or specialized vocabulary that need to be learned as part of a course (like idioms or aviation terminology). Another example might see screencasts being used to present new vocabulary using an audio- or video-based flash card method with one student saying the word and the other giving the definition, and trading off on this procedure as they record. A further example is flipping the classroom, where content is first introduced and learned through a podcast or screencast for homework, with time in class spent on practice and review.

Podcasts and screencasts can also be used by teachers to cover content that is necessary, but these are more suitable for review outside of class time (for example, grammar points, or functions of language), leaving the classroom free for speaking and other more targeted activities. Students themselves could also be tasked with creating podcasts and screencasts that go over such points as well as essential vocabulary, and even be responsible for summarizing classroom content for later examination review and for peers who have missed a class. Screencasting students can annotate their work as they show it on screen, and, depending on the software used for editing, include interactive quizzes for completion. In either case, students who are responsible for developing podcasts and screencasts can begin to take control of the learning process, and this can lead to higher motivation. It also allows them to produce content that can then form part of a digital portfolio, and material that can then be assessed based on student performance – rather than continually provided work that is teacher-delivered.

Teachers may wish to record parts or the whole of their classroom activities as a live screencast or podcast over the course of a year or term, and they will have material that is reusable and ready to archive after editing. In this way, teachers who are taxed for time can still begin to develop content with minimal production time involved. However, those teachers that do have more time could specifically record mini-lectures, or short 'show-and-tells' to present the main points covered by each class or unit, and provide a personalized example of the format of work expected to be produced by students. An example of this for a speech class sees the teacher write a small speech using the model available to students from their textbooks, but personalizing it with content from their own life when conducting the screencast. In this manner, the teacher will have students engaged with content on a very different level from any text or any accompanying publisher video. This kind of podcast or screencast not only provides additional material for review, but it provides an increased connection to the teacher along with development of multimodal learning. For distance learners, or those engaged in blended or online learning, establishing a personal connection with the teacher through just such content can be important for continued study success.

Further, teachers when providing feedback or advice on student submissions can use podcasts and screencasts. In conversation, or in speaking classes, teachers can note any student errors and mistakes made throughout the week, and provide examples of usage in a mini-podcast that can be assigned for out-of-class listening each week. It is podcasts like these that could also be retasked for use as in-class activities, with work sheets and additional tasks set in conjunction. In writing classes on the other hand, students can submit work digitally and, rather than using tools that track changes when editing these submissions, teachers could use a screencast to provide personalized descriptive feedback. This kind of feedback is made by recording the screen and verbalizing any explanations, corrections, comments, and annotations made to students work, while simultaneously highlighting any points of note (both excellent and poor) as you go. All of this can be conducted in what would normally be set aside as grading time anyway. This particular kind of screencast could be applied to virtually any kind of digitally submitted work (like essays, infographics, and slideshows), and provides a way to add a more personalized touch and an additional means of establishing a connection with students over that usually obtained via rubrics or comments written on assignments.

7

How can I start using podcasts and screencasts with students?

There are a great number of sources from where to begin looking for podcasts and screencasts to use in the classroom. When accessing these sources it might also be helpful to look at content from one of three different perspectives: traditional, expert, and classroom.

Traditional content

Traditional content can be provided to students as audio or video recorded material for students to use to catch up if they have missed lessons, or for students to use as a review of any classroom introduced content. Examples might include providing resource links to TOEFL test podcasts or screencasts, or links to podcasts and screencasts that cover the kind of grammar points or language focus introduced by the weekly topic or unit.

Expert content

Expert content can easily be retasked or used directly as supplementary material for homework or alongside textbook content, and this can be in the form of amateurs interviewing experts or the experts themselves talking or presenting on a particular topic. If teaching English for specific purposes (ESP), or general English to medical majors at college level, this might include finding podcasts and screencasts on health topics where specialist doctors are interviewed on the topic areas that are also touched on by the class textbooks.

Classroom content

Classroom content is where students and the teachers themselves would begin to produce their own material as podcasts and screencasts which would see students beginning to share specific insights into their learning, critique completed tasks, activities, or peer work, and engage in a variety of production techniques that could potentially lead to language practice and linguistic development. Examples could then be shared to the internet and redistributed to all learners in the form of a podcast or screencast.

Accessing sources

A variety of podcasts and screencasts are readily available for incorporation into the classroom, and to be used as a means to augment lesson content. These include those focusing on elements such as: English for specific purposes (like business English and medical English); current affairs topics; grammar topics; idioms; slang; songs; vocabulary; and much more. Sources for gaining access to a range of podcasts and screencasts on different topics and genres like these, aside from conducting a search on iTunes or Google, include the following:

ESLPod provides a range of podcast content tailored to second-language learners of English, from specific topics through to test taking guides.

Podcast Alley is the place to go if you want to find out the latest news about podcasts, and to gain access to the top podcasts.

QT-ESL Podcasts provides a range of podcasts that cover oral grammar practice, and which include scripts and worksheets.

TED Talks provide talks of various lengths in a presentation video format that is given by experts.

YouTube provides a great deal of user-generated content, and also a large number of screencasts and the opportunity to subscribe to channels.

Accessing content

In order to begin using podcasts and screencasts with learners, students will need to know how to download or subscribe to them, how to listen to them or how to view them, and how to gain access to any podcast show notes or screencast program notes that are available. In most cases, you as the teacher will be able to provide the necessary web links to the content that you require your students to view or hear, but if you are using a particular podcast or screencast channel consistently, then you may need to show your students how to subscribe to the appropriate content provider. If you want them to develop their own podcasts and screencasts, you will certainly need to provide materials and tutorials to teach them how to plan and produce this kind of content (perhaps by developing a podcast or screencast yourself) as well as developing or gaining access to a rubric to evaluate final products.

8

How do I evaluate podcasts and screencasts?

Perhaps the most appropriate means available to evaluate a podcast or a screencast, particularly in the TESOL context, is to use a prefabricated rubric based upon a Likert-type rating scale. Any such rubric should be presented to students beforehand, so that they can understand what will be expected from them and what will be assessed.

Evaluation rubrics, particularly those using indicators across several categories, are essential when assessing the quality of student work on any complex multimedia-based project. Although it is useful for the busy teacher to apply pre-made rubrics, it is better if teachers formulate their own that reflect their teaching environment and the points that they wish to assess. One good source for this is Rubistar, where there are a number of pre-made evaluation options as well as information on how to create unique context sensitive evaluation instruments. The rubrics section of the resources list also contains several other rubric creation tools that may prove worthwhile to look over.

Here are three sample rubrics that can be used with students in any classroom, including those participating in podcast or screencast production from within the TESOL setting. The first focuses on podcasts in terms of student planning, production, and publishing, the second focuses on the planning, production, and publishing of a screencast, while the third looks at providing a means for assessing the quality of student produced scripts or narrations intended for use in the production stage of a podcast or screencast.

The rating scale used in the following rubrics go from 1 to 5, with 1 being poor, 2 fair, 3 average, 4 good, and 5 excellent. 'Average' is used as a midpoint so that students can see how each particular skill relates to peers. This allows teachers to identify the skills that are weak in individual students, and those that can be improved.

38 | P o d c a s t i n g   a n d   s c r e e n c a s t i n g

Podcasts – Student developed

Assessment Item	Assessment Criteria	Score
Introduction	Tells the audience who the podcaster is, the date and location, and what to expect.	1 2 3 4 5
Content	Clear purpose, and a constant focus placed on presenting the topic to the audience.	1 2 3 4 5
Delivery	The show flows well with a conversational tone maintained; volume of the voice is constant.	1 2 3 4 5
Language	Specialized vocabulary and grammar are used correctly; definitions are provided.	1 2 3 4 5
Conclusion	Clearly summarizes key points, directs listener towards show notes, and invites participation.	1 2 3 4 5
Technical	The podcast is of a good length, transitions are well-timed, sound levels are consistent, and everything is audible.	1 2 3 4 5
Show Notes	All resources mentioned are included, and access to the notes is easily available.	1 2 3 4 5
Group Work	All people in the group had a role, and participated equally toward the finished product.	1 2 3 4 5

Ratings: 1 Poor 2 Fair 3 Average 4 Good 5 Excellent

Screencasts – Student developed

Assessment Item	Assessment Criteria	Score
Introduction	Topic overview provided, and expectations set.	1 2 3 4 5
Content	Clear purpose, and a constant focus placed on presenting the explanation to the audience.	1 2 3 4 5
Delivery	Screencast flows well, with a conversational tone maintained.	1 2 3 4 5
Language	Specialized vocabulary and grammar are used correctly; definitions are provided.	1 2 3 4 5
Conclusion	Clearly summarizes key points, directs listeners towards program notes, and invites subscriber participation.	1 2 3 4 5
Technical	Transitions are smooth; sound levels are consistent; everything is audible. Annotations, callouts, captions, and zooms are appropriate, and add value.	1 2 3 4 5
Program Notes (if included)	All additional resources or links mentioned are included, and access to notes is available.	1 2 3 4 5
Group Work	All people in the group had a role, and participated equally toward the finished product.	1 2 3 4 5

Ratings: 1 Poor 2 Fair 3 Average 4 Good 5 Excellent

Podcasts and Screencasts – Script/Narration

Assessment Item	Assessment Criteria	Score
Introduction	Provides relevant information.	1 2 3 4 5
	Establishes a clear purpose, and states the objectives of the podcast/screencast.	1 2 3 4 5
	Engages with the audience.	1 2 3 4 5
Content	Creative and original content that enhances the topic(s).	1 2 3 4 5
	Well-researched, with all information accurate and informative.	1 2 3 4 5
	The direction of the show (podcast topics or screencast explanations) follows a logical sequence.	1 2 3 4 5
Podcasts only	Well-edited 'questions' for experts or guests, with potential for follow-up.	1 2 3 4 5
Screencasts only	Well-edited 'quotes' from experts, credited appropriately.	1 2 3 4 5
Language	Vocabulary enhances content, grammar is used correctly.	1 2 3 4 5
Show/Program Notes	Resource links are all functional, and appropriate.	1 2 3 4 5
	Everything is cited, or credited correctly if not copyright free.	1 2 3 4 5

Ratings: 1 Poor 2 Fair 3 Average 4 Good 5 Excellent

9

What tools are available for podcast and screencast production?

There are a number of commercial and free applications available to create podcasts and screencasts, and more examples are provided in the podcasting, interactive whiteboard, and screencasting sections of the resources list. Some of these tools are expensive, while others are free. Purely online editing tools have become available as well as app-based tools for Android and IOS devices. Here are some of the most notable.

Audacity is a free multi-track audio recorder and editor that contains some very powerful features, including those for adding effects to files and conducting analysis of the audio recorded. It is one of the most popular tools for podcasting.

Garage Band is available for Apple products, and can be used to create audio-only and enhanced podcasts.

Pod-O-Matic allows for the upload of audio and video files, from either a computer or from a media library on another device, for hosting on their servers.

FeedForAll allows for the creation, editing, and publishing of RSS feeds.

Feedity is an online tool to create an RSS feed for any webpage, and there is an option to upgrade to a premium account that offers additional features.

FetchRSS: RSS Generator is an online RSS feed generator that can create a feed out of almost any webpage, automatically update the RSS feed when new content is added to the page, and generate an RSS feed for a social networking site.

Screenchomp allows users to annotate pictures or to use the application as a whiteboard. Any work completed with the application can be saved automatically to the internet.

Screencast-O-Matic offers 15 minutes of install-free branded recording time for the free version, or 60-minutes recording time for the branding-free paid version. Any created screencast can be saved locally to their server, or to YouTube.

TechSmith Camtasia Studio is one of the most comprehensive screencasting editing tools available, and provides a great deal of control over the creation process. It also has a great range of extensive features including a large number of transitions, zoom effects, and noise reduction capabilities. Files can be saved in a variety of formats both locally and to the internet (for example, screencast.com and YouTube). It has a higher learning curve than other tools have, and although it is on the more expensive side for many educators, it is one of the most popular and comprehensive screencasting tools on the market.

10

How do I plan and produce a podcast or a screencast?

Planning a podcast or screencast

Once the tools to create and distribute a podcast or screencast have been selected, the pre-production, production, and post-production aspects of development can be considered. To this end, the following steps will assist.

Podcasting

A potential model to follow when planning out the development of a podcast is as follows: planning → producing → publishing → promoting.

Planning

Starting out podcasting, either as a teacher or getting students to create their own, is best done by creating one that is shorter (say, five-minutes) rather than longer. Whatever the length, developing a podcast involves the need for planning to meet the intent of the broadcast. There needs to be an outline, if only to determine if there needs to be one long episode or a series of shorter episodes. The style of the recording (audio or video) needs to be chosen, along with a quite location to maximize the recording quality.

Producing

For this component of podcast creation, the hardware and software needs to be obtained. At a minimum, there needs to be a suitable computer, microphone, and audio recording software. A web camera or screencasting software will also be required for a video podcast.

Publishing

The podcast will need to be uploaded to a hosting service, and an RSS feed created to distribute the episode. Show notes and links to various resources discussed in the podcast will need to be hosted on a site or made available for download.

Promoting

An effective means to promote the podcast is to get listeners and guests to suggest future topics, ask questions, suggest other guests to interview, and take part in contests. In addition, links to the podcast feed and show notes, and behind-the-scene photos, can be spread across various social media sites like Facebook and Twitter.

Screencasting

Potential steps to follow when considering the development of a screencast are: topic → objectives → format → scripting → capturing → editing → publishing → promoting.

Topic

Select the unit or lesson that will be covered.

Objectives

Determine the learning objectives based on the selected unit or lesson.

Format

Determine the screencast format based on the unit or lesson covered, and in light of the lesson objectives (for example, demonstration, presentation, tutorial).

Scripting

Walk through the steps on screen that you intend to discuss in the screencast, type out a script as you go, and read through the script before beginning any recording to determine the timing. Keep both the needs of the viewer and the prepared objectives in mind, and keep language to that of an everyday conversational tone.

Capturing

Decide on the area of the screen that will be recorded. Any narration or script can either be recorded live or added in post-production so that it matches with on-screen activity, but this will depend on the software being used. Callouts and zooming, along with various other effects, can also be added when editing, but they do need to be considered at this stage. Keep on topic, don't get distracted, and don't be afraid to pause the recording to rest or take a sip of water if needed. Speak clearly and slow enough for viewers to be able to follow along easily.

Editing

After recording the screencast, a variety of media can be edited in to enhance the recording from the narration itself through to additional animations, music, photos, and video clips. Other features such as zooming or callouts to grab attention and orient the focus can also be added. Less is more – edit to capture only what the viewer needs to see, and leave the rest on the 'cutting room floor'.

Publishing

After finalizing the editing process, the screencast can be saved as a movie file or uploaded to a YouTube channel or a learning management system (LMS), or it can be distributed for in-class delivery.

Promoting

The audience of your screencast will depend on how you promote it, and a class blog or class website will ensure that various stakeholders will also be able to gain access to any developed content once the screencast is published. Screencasts can also become evidence of classroom activities and form part of a portfolio for both the teacher and the students.

Producing a podcast or screencast

There are several steps that are unique to podcast and screencast production – no matter what hardware or software is being used to record them, and no matter where associated links and show notes will be hosted, the feed used for any distribution, or any social media sites used for promotion. The length of both podcasts and screencasts should be based on the selected topic, interest, or points under review or presentation, but they need to maintain continuity whatever their length, with the minimum being five to six minutes (for example, when reviewing a point or discussing a shorter topic). They can be for an hour or more (for example, when a class is recorded, a tutorial provided, or a specialist is interviewed). Here are some example production steps, associated timings and comments on the process involved.

Podcasting production steps

Introductory music (30-60 seconds)

Play a unique identifier for your show that audience members can associate with you. This can then lead into the podcast, with the introduction monolog as a voice-over.

Introductory monologue (30-60 seconds)

State who you are, introduce any guests, and state the topics to be discussed.

Topics (3-5 minutes each)

Stay focused on the key aspects of the topic by asking guests a specific question (or posing questions to yourself), and guiding guests back on track where necessary. It is advisable to prepare a script for solo podcasts. Throughout each topic, remind the listener that any resources or links will be posted as show notes, and where these can be obtained.

Closing remarks (2 minutes)

Thank the audience for listening, thank any guests, mention the topic and/or guests of the next show, and remind the audience where to go for show notes.

Closing music (2 minutes)

Play out the podcast with the same music track as used in the introduction. This can be started during the closing remarks and continue afterwards.

Screencasting production steps

Introduction (30-60 seconds)

Select the screen area that will become the focus, and provide a voice-over introduction to the topic or topics that will be discussed, with an overview of the steps involved.

Topics (3-5 minutes each)

Each topic-based section needs to stay on script, keep the viewer informed, and tell them everything that you are doing. Zoom into and highlight features only when they are being discussed, use annotations and callouts where necessary, and edit out any pauses or mistakes in post-production.

Closing remarks (2 minutes)
Finish off by thanking the viewers, and reminding them of the topics covered, the knowledge and skills that have been imparted by watching the screencast, and how these skills can now be put to use.

11

How would I use a tool to produce and publish a podcast and a screencast?

To begin podcasting or screencasting, several technological tools are necessary. Typically for podcasts, typically a device capable of running audio recording software and possessing a built-in microphone would be the minimum required. For screencasting, access to a device capable of running screen recording software and recording audio, and that has a built-in web camera, is the minimum. Software that has the ability to highlight the mouse location, create zoom effects, and create on-screen annotations (like callouts and text), along with an external microphone, should be considered. Places to publish the final product need also be taken into account. For podcasts this might involve the development of RSS feeds and a place to host transcripts and show notes such as a blogging site, while screencasts may be uploaded to a YouTube channel with program notes and a transcript posted in the description. To assist in developing a transcript to include, along with show and program notes, voice recognition software would be required. To begin either podcasting or screencasting, you will need the hardware, the software, the time, and the topic. Rather than focusing on providing a tutorial for the use of each software item required, the focus here will be placed more on the steps involved when going about publishing and promoting a podcast or screencast.

11A. Podcasts

Preparation

To produce a studio-quality podcast, you will need access to several resources:

- A device capable of recording and saving your episodes.
- An external microphone, along with a pop filter or pop shield, is strongly recommended, although a built-in microphone could be used.
- An application to record your voice and to save the file for editing and file conversation.
- A voice-recognition application to convert your audio file to written text, or to perform the conversion in real-time, so that subscribers will be able to access a transcript of the podcast.
- A text editing application to edit the transcript, and show notes.
- An image editing application to create your cover art.
- A site to host your podcast file, transcript, images, and show notes.

- An application to create an RSS feed of your podcast.
- A plan to publish and promote your RSS feed across multiple platforms.

Step One – Content development

The first step in creating a podcast is to plan it out, and then produce it, and the steps involved in this process have already been outlined. You should also be familiar with any copyright issues that may impact your broadcast. Once you have recorded your MP3 or MP4 file, then you can begin to edit it, trimming silences, and any mistakes or periods of awkwardness.

Step Two – Transcription

To start to convert a podcast episode into a transcript, the use of voice-recognition software like Dragon Naturally Speaking would be ideal, but for a short podcast, it could be done manually. The transcript should be saved in PDF file format, and no matter how it is generated, be sure to read through the transcript to ensure that it is correct and error free.

You will then need to tidy it up so that it reflects your podcast appropriately, and this includes adding pertinent information to the file such as the podcast title, air date, images, most certainly identifying who is saying what and when, and when each section starts (for example, identifying each new topic discussed).

Step Three – Show notes

One you have a transcript, you will be able to search through it for keywords, so that you can begin to generate links to all the resources, applications, products, and whatever else was mentioned in the show. If you have identified all of the items to be included in show notes with an audible tag (like the phrase 'show notes') as you recorded your podcast, then this will be a relatively easy task to perform. The show notes should contain all the appropriate details associated with the podcast episode (for example, title, air dates, and images) to identify your podcast.

Step Four – Cover art

You will need to create a JPG or PNG file to use as the cover art, or a podcast album cover, of your podcast. The image file should be a minimum of 1400 x 1400 pixels and a maximum of 3000 x 3000 pixels, and it should also be clear when scaled down to a size of 50 x 50 pixels. You might decide to use a photograph and overlay the name of the podcast on the photo, but remember that this image will become representative of your podcast to all of your subscribers. If interested, a number of example images can be seen on the cover art of the podcasts found at the podgallery website. At this point, you should also perform a search to confirm that the name of your podcast is unique before you begin to find a hosting provider.

Step Five – Hosting

After you have all of your podcast files complete, you will then need to find a place to host or store them (the audio/video podcast file itself, the transcript, the show notes, associated images, and so on). A number of places exist for free hosting, including blogging sites like WordPress.

Step Six – Posting and tagging

WordPress has built in support for podcasts while a number of other platforms do not. It is advisable to create a new page with a new domain to be used as your feed, and WordPress allows for a number of domains and sites to be included under the one username. To create a podcast post after creating your site, generate a normal blog post and tag it with the keyword 'podcast'. After that, use the WYSIWYG (What you see is what you get) editor to add all your podcast files and to create the content, look, and the hyperlinks that will point to all your podcast episode files. It is this URL that will be used to create the RSS feed.

Step Seven – Feeding the podcast

To publish a podcast to iTunes or other places so that people can search and subscribe to it, you will need an RSS feed, and you can create this with a number of sites, from FeedBurner through to FETCHRSS: RSS

Generator. For now, to use FETCHRSS: RSS Generator, or simply FetchRSS, you will need to register. A free service is provided which allows for a feed limit of five, is updated daily, and shows the last five updates with text-based ads. The free service would be sufficient for many teachers, as the feeds are deleted if no one is reading them after seven days, but it also has a paid service. It should be noted that you can use any web page to create a feed.

Step Eight – Creating the feed

To create your first feed automatically, go to the FetchRSS website, enter the URL of the webpage you would like to convert into a feed, and then click 'Continue'. You will then be taken to some subscription options, of which the free plan would be the most suitable to select at this time. After that, you will be able to click 'Go to my RSS list' where you will be able to see each feed or link that you have converted into an RSS feed. You will also be able to download the RSS feeds as outline processor markup language (OPML). The OPML file is useful as it can hold all your RSS subscription information for backup and sharing. Although not required, you could also use an application called Feedly to import your OMPL file, or use the online application OPML Viewer to view the contents of the file. The code of each feed can also be read by clicking on the name of the feed.

Step Nine – Configuring the feed

From the 'My RSS list' page, you will have several configuration options that include 'Settings' from where you can change your login data, and 'Plan' from where you can select a paid subscription as well as options for configuring, disabling, deleting, or reading your feed with any aggregator. You also have the option to access a 'manual RSS builder' if you would like to go that route. Click on 'Config' to change the details associated with a feed, such as the title, description, and the number of news items in the feed. Click on 'Disable' to disable the feed, 'Enable' to enable it at a later time, and select one of the other options to get the feed in other formats, including Atom (an XML syndication format), CSV (for use with spreadsheet programs), or JSON (Java Script Object

Notation). If you no longer want to keep the feed, click 'Delete' to remove it from the list.

Step Ten – Publishing and promoting the feed

One of the most popular vehicles for podcast distribution and discovery is iTunes, and there are other options including Google Play Music (depending on geographical location) and places like SoundCloud. To submit your RSS feed to iTunes, you will need to go to 'iTunes connect', sign in with an Apple ID, and provide your RSS feed for validation. If approved, your podcast will be listed in the iTunes directory, but if not, you can still use your RSS feed on any of your PDF files (including the transcript and the show notes), and promote your podcast across a range of other platforms (for example, Facebook, your blog, and your email signature). Clicking on the feed would open a listener's favorite news aggregator into which they would be able to download and listen to all (yes, all) of your podcasts. You should also provide this information as a 'Call to action' at the close of your podcast, telling your listeners how and where to subscribe so they can automatically receive any future podcasts that you produce.

11B. Screencasts

Preparation

To produce a high-end screencast you will need access to several resources:

- A device capable of running screen recording software and of recording audio.

- An external microphone with a pop filter or pop shield is strongly recommended, although a built-in microphone could be used.

- A web camera, if you wish to record yourself as you provide a voiceover.

- An application capable of recording on-screen applications as well as audio.

- An application to edit your recording and capable of highlighting mouse location and creating zoom effects and on-screen annotations such as callouts and text is highly recommended.

- A voice recognition application to convert the audio of your recording to written text, or to perform the conversion in real-time, so that subscribers will be able to access a transcript of the screencast.

- A text editing application to edit the transcript and program notes.

- An image editing application to create your channel art.

- A site to host your screencast channel, where you will upload your files, transcripts, and program notes, and from where your viewers can subscribe.

- A plan to promote your screencasts and channels across multiple platforms.

Step One – Content development

The first step in creating a webcast is to plan it out, and then produce it. The ways to do this have already been outlined, and you should also be familiar with any copyright issues that may impact your broadcast. Once you have recorded your MP4 file, then you can add additional items of focus, such as annotations, callouts, and zoom effects, and edit out any silences, mistakes, or periods of awkwardness.

Step Two – Transcription

To start to convert a screencast into a transcript, the use of voice recognition software like Dragon Naturally Speaking would be ideal, otherwise for a shorter screencast, it could be done manually. The emerging transcript should then be saved in PDF file format, but be sure to read through the transcript to ensure that it is correct and error free. You will then need to tidy it up so that it reflects your screencast appropriately. This would include adding pertinent information to the file such as the screencast title, air date, images, and when each section starts (for example, new topics and applications being discussed) starts.

Step Three – Program notes

One you have a transcript, you will be able to search through it for keywords so that you can generate links to all the resources, applications, products, and the other things that are mentioned in the screencast. If you have identified all of the items to be included in program notes with an audible tag (like 'program notes') as you recorded your screencast, then this will be relatively easy. The program notes should contain all of the appropriate details associated with the screencast episode (for example, the title and air dates), along with any associated images that identify your screencast.

Step Four – Channel art
Although channel art is not necessarily required, it is a good idea to use it as an identifier for your screencasts (perhaps at the beginning and end of all your episodes). In this case, you would need to create an image file with dimensions of 2560 x 1440 pixels, and no larger than 4 MB. You may decide to use a photograph, and overlay the name of the screencast on the photo. Remember that this image will become representative of your screencast to all of your subscribers.

Step Five – Hosting
After you have all of your screencast files complete, you will then need to find a place to host or store them (like the screencast video file itself, the transcript, the program notes, and associated images).

A number of places exist for hosting video files including YouTube, TechSmith Screencast.com, and Vimeo where you can also include hyperlinks to external files hosted on sites such as WordPress, and provide a link back to your screencast.

Step Six – Channeling screencasts

On YouTube, you can create a channel with a unique name for your screencast, and link this to a Google+ page of the same name. This allows for management from a single account. The upload and conversion process of videos may take some time, after which you will be able to edit them from the 'Video manager'. Links added to the 'About' page of your channel will also be featured below your channel description, and they can include one to your website, one to your podcast, and others to social media like Facebook, Twitter, or Instagram.

Step Seven – Channel video editing

Once your screencast is hosted or uploaded onto YouTube, you will be able to see it from the 'Video manager'. Clicking on the 'Edit' button to the right of each video that you have uploaded provides you with a variety of editing options that include: general information and settings (including titles and descriptions), enhancements (such as stabilization, filters, and blurring of faces), audio (where you can choose ad-free tracks as background music), annotations (where you can overlay text on the video), cards (which can be used to overlay clickable hyperlinks on the video), and subtitles (where you can upload your transcription for use as this feature).

Step Eight – Carding, annotating, and subtitling channel videos

Perhaps the most important features on offer for a TESOL screencaster relying on YouTube as a channel provider are the 'Annotation', 'Card' and 'Subtitle' features of the 'Video manager'.

The 'Annotation' tab allows you to add a 'Title', 'Notes', and 'Speech bubbles', and to 'Label' or 'Spotlight' an area. All of these, aside from the 'Title' allow you to also add a hyperlink to a 'Video', a 'Playlist', a 'Channel', a 'Crowdfunding project', and most importantly to 'Subscription' where you can help people subscribe to your channel or to others.

The 'Card' tab also provides a series of overlay options that include the ability to add an information card to promote a 'Video or playlist', promote another 'Channel', 'Link' to an external website, or involve subscribers by encouraging them to participate in a multiple-choice 'Poll'. The poll feature can be used to ask review questions of students as the video progresses, and these questions can tie with any worksheets for later classes or for post-viewing. Additional annotations can be added to suit different classes that might require links to different content from the same material, or are learning different points from the same content. This allows for reusability of any created screencast with different levels of language learners.

Finally, the 'Subtitle' tab will allow you to import your transcript and sync it with your video. This feature can be turned off and on, and may prove useful depending on the level of second-language learner that you are teaching. It is also a useful feature that will allow learners to continue watching your screencasts if they do not have headphones, and are in public places (such as a library) where they will need to mute their device.

Step Nine – Feeding the screencast

To further promote your screencasts, you can, as with a podcast, rely on an RSS feed, and you can create this with a number of sites from FeedBurner through to FETCHRSS: RSS Generator. For now, using FETCHRSS: RSS Generator, or simply FetchRSS, you will need to register. A free service is provided which allows for a feed limit of five, is updated daily, and shows the last five updates with text-based ads. The free service would be sufficient for many teachers as the feeds are deleted if no one is reading them after seven days, but there is also a paid service. It should be noted that you can use any URL or webpage to create a feed.

Step Ten – Creating the feed

To create your first feed automatically, go to the FetchRSS website, and enter the URL of the webpage that you would like to convert into a feed, then click 'Continue'. You will then be taken to some subscription options, and the free plan would be the most suitable to select at this time. When you click 'Go to my RSS list', you can then see each feed or link that you have converted into an RSS feed. You will also be able to download the RSS feeds as outline processor markup language (OPML). The OPML file is useful as it can hold all your RSS subscription information for backup and sharing. Although not required, you could also use an application that imports your OPML file, or use the online application OPML Viewer to view the contents of the file. The code of each feed can also be read by clicking on the name of the feed.

Step Eleven – Configuring the feed

From the 'My RSS list' page, you have several configuration options that include 'Settings' (from where you can change your login data), and 'Plan' (from where you can select a paid subscription), as well as options for configuring, disabling, deleting, or reading your feed on FeedHub (an online News Aggregator). You also have the option to access the 'Manual RSS builder' if you would like to go that route. Click on 'Config' to change the details associated with a feed such as the title, description, and the number of news items in the feed. Click on 'Disable' to disable the feed, 'Enable' to enable it at a later time, and select one of the other options to get the feed in other formats, including Atom (an XML syndication format), CSV (for use with spreadsheet programs), or JSON (Java Script Object Notation). If you no longer want to keep the feed, click 'Delete' to remove it from the list.

Step Twelve – Publishing and promoting the feed and channel

One of the most popular vehicles for podcast distribution and discovery is iTunes, and along with places like YouTube, it can also be used to host your screencasting content. To submit your RSS feed to iTunes, you will need to go to 'iTunes connect' and sign in with an Apple ID, and after that, you will be able to provide your RSS feed for validation. If approved, your screencast will be listed in the iTunes directory, but if not, you can still use your RSS feed on any of your PDF files (including the transcript and the program notes), and promote your screencast across a range of other platforms (for example, Facebook, your blog, and your email signature). Clicking on the feed would open a listener's favorite news aggregator into which they would be able to download and watch *all* of your screencasts. You should also provide this information as a 'Call to action' at the close of your screencast, and by telling your viewer to click on the 'Subscribe' button to your channel if hosting your screencasts on YouTube.

12

What are the key points behind podcast and screencast use in the TESOL context?

A variety of key points associated with podcasts and screencasts that are important to keep in mind when using the technology with language learners include the following:

- Podcasting and screencasting offer new ways to provide traditional learning content through the transmediation of content, and offer innovative and creative ways to perform traditional tasks.
- Podcasts and screencasts allow for the narrowcasting of content, and for time- and place-shifting of its consumption.
- Podcasts can prove appealing to students who prefer auditory-based learning, and to those who do not like to read or may have problems with reading. Screencasts may appeal to those same students, as well as those who prefer aurally and visually oriented learning material.

- Both podcasting and screencasting provide the opportunity to encourage active and targeted learning.

- Teacher-produced episodes should be kept short and on point, focusing on learner needs, particularly if flipping the lesson. Clarification can be undertaken in class.

- A number of sources are available for podcast and download subscription as well as applications for their development. The type of content that can be produced can stem from traditional material (textbooks and the set curriculum), the expert (a guest lecturer), and the classroom (student generated content).

- Engaging students in episode production leads to listening skills practice, concentration on speaking with attention to speed, pronunciation, and clarity of voice in particular.

- Planning a podcast or screencast requires listening and discussion while collaborating as well as reading and writing while constructing the production plan itself.

- Multiple literacies, along with other essential skills (for example, research, time-management, and problem-solving) can be developed through episode production and subscription.
- The four main types of podcast are solo, interview, multi-host, and video. The four main types of screencast are presentation, demonstration, streaming, and whiteboarding.
- Thoughtful and careful editing, along with thorough planning, are key to good development. Keeping on topic, staying focused, and highlighting key information is also important.
- Involving subscribers is another aspect that is important. Posing questions, asking them to leave comments, and replying to those comments creates interaction.
- Program or show notes need developing, and they are essential in providing both a summary for the episode along with links to further resources for those interested.

- Evaluation should be done with comprehensive rubrics. Take into account all sides of development: planning, production, and publishing.

In a world where content is increasingly required for just-in-time learning, and knowledge essentially needed only on demand, podcasting and screencasting find themselves extremely conducive for learning. They also offer innovative and creative ways of providing education to students, with episode use and production allowing for the development of a broad range of essential life-skills as well as the practice of key second-language skills. This is particularly poignant for the TESOL context as a means of meeting the immediate needs of students by providing targeted instruction, and would come to enhance the learning experience of all involved.

13
Lesson plan guides, and example implementation

Provided here are lesson plan guides, as well as an example for implementing podcasts and screencasts in the educational context. The guides are meant to assist in the understanding of how to develop a detailed lesson plan, and to help describe what each component and stage of a lesson may cover. The example implementations are intended to provide a use-case scenario detailing the techniques required to apply the use of podcasts and screencasts in real-world settings.

The content covered here includes:
- Lesson plan general guide
- Lesson plan guide for podcasting
- Example implementation: Podcasting
- Lesson plan guide for screencasting
- Example implementation: Screencasting

Lesson Plan General Guide	
Teaching Context	
Level of Proficiency and Maturity	Student language level (e.g. beginner, intermediate, advanced). Student age range (e.g. young learners, adults).
Lesson Length	Time allotted for the class (e.g. 35-45 minutes).
Lesson Topic	Major theme or focus of the lesson (e.g. numbers and time).
Objectives	Lesson aim (e.g. to teach students how to tell the time and date accurately).
Outcomes	Learning outcomes (e.g. students will be able to read analog and digital timepieces).
Relevant Prior Learning	Anything that students need to know before starting work on this lesson's content (e.g. students need to have completed Chapter Two of the book, and have previously met language associated with appointments, calendars, and timekeeping).

Teacher Preparation	
Hardware	Types of computer or peripherals required (e.g. USB sticks, MP3 players).
Software	Name of software used (e.g. Photo Story 3, Microsoft Word).
Webpage Links	Hyperlink to web resources (e.g. www.google.com).
Additional Resources	Other necessary materials for the lesson (e.g. handouts, worksheets, textbooks).

Procedure			
Stage and Timing	Objective	Teacher	Students
Review Stage (if required, 5 minutes)	Focus of stage (e.g. encourage the use of previously acquired language).	Indicate what the teacher says and does in each stage of the lesson.	Provide expected examples of student behavior.

Warm-up Stage/Pre-Technology Use (10 minutes)	Focus of stage (e.g. introduce new concepts and language to students in a meaningful manner).	Indicate what the teacher says and does in each stage of the lesson.	Provide expected examples of student behavior.
Main Stage/ Technology-based Activity (20 minutes)	Focus of stage (e.g. allow students to utilize technology to become familiar with and apply the concepts and language content introduced in the lesson).	Indicate what the teacher says and does in each stage of the lesson.	Provide expected examples of student behavior.

Practice Stage (15 minutes)	Focus of stage (e.g. allow learners to utilize the skills and language that they are expected to acquire during the lesson in a practical way).	Indicate what the teacher says and does in each stage of the lesson.	Provide expected examples of student behavior.
Lesson Summation Stage/Post-Technology Activities (10 minutes)	Focus of stage (e.g. instructor reinforces the importance of language concepts and skills acquired, stating how they will be useful in forthcoming lessons).	Indicate what the teacher says and does in each stage of the lesson.	Provide expected examples of student behavior.

Further Considerations	
Follow-Up Activities	Prepare material that can be applied in a follow up class. Also, be ready with activities for students who complete their class work earlier than expected.
Contingency Plan(s)	Always prepare an alternate teaching scenario in case of any problems. For example, a sudden power outage, or a timetabling issue could make the assigned room unavailable.
Evaluation	Reflect on what worked well, and what did not, and how you might deliver the lesson differently or improve upon it when running it again.

Lesson Plan Guide for Podcasting	
Teaching Context	
Level of Proficiency and Maturity	Beginner to advanced. Adaptable for use with young learners through to adults.
Lesson Length	Suitable for several lessons over a week. Homework completion components. Time allotted for each class: 50 minutes.
Lesson Topic	Variable, anything suited to a commercial radio broadcast would work well, particularly talkback interviews.
Objectives	1. Enhance communication skills through collaborative learning, asking questions, expressing opinions, and developing scripts. 2. Strengthen multiple literacies (computer literacy, digital literacy, and English literacy).
Outcomes	1. Students identify significant questions on a topic, and use these in interview format. 2. Transfer current knowledge into learning, using and understanding technological systems.
Relevant Prior Learning	None required. Screencasting or digital storytelling familiarity helpful.

Teacher Preparation	
Hardware	Computer or tablet with audio recording capability (e.g. built-in or external microphone). USB sticks or Google Drive for storage.
Software	Podcasting software (e.g. Audacity).
Webpage Links	podgallery.org
Additional Resources	Handouts*: • Podcast summary and review • Podcast design plan • Podcasting production plan • Podcast show notes

*Available under 'Photocopiable content'.

Procedure – Day 1 of 3			
Stage and Timing	Objective	Teacher	Students
Introductory Stage (5 minutes)	Determine student familiarity with podcasts, and find out what students like to listen to on the radio.	Determine student familiarity with podcasts by introducing radio shows, and downloadable and streaming programs (e.g. from Podgallery, or other sources).	Express opinions about the radio shows that they like to listen to, download or stream.
Warm-up Stage/Pre-Technology Use (5 minutes)	Brainstorm good topics for podcasts, and provide links to examples of suitable podcasts.	Help students think of topics that they can later use to make their own podcasts, and provide links to suitable examples.	Students start to think about topics that are suitable for podcasts, and they are introduced to some that they can listen to later.

Main Stage (20 minutes)	Play an interview type podcast to students, suitable to their language level.	Play a short podcast to students, at a maximum of three times, and have them complete the 'Podcast Summary and Review' handout*.	Students will listen to the podcast, and complete the associated handout.
Lesson Summation Stage/Post-Technology Activities (10 minutes)	Go through the worksheet answers with students, and remind them of podcasts that are suitable for language learning.	Go over the worksheet with students, and check answers. Finish the lesson by providing several podcast links for students to listen to in their own time.	Students are called on to provide their answers from the worksheet, and are provided with suitable podcast links that they can use to improve their English.

*Available under 'Photocopiable content'.

Procedure – Day 2 of 3			
Stage and Timing	Objective	Teacher	Students
Review Stage **(5 minutes)**	Remind students of podcasts, types of podcasts, and the structure of a podcast.	Introduce the structure of podcasts by talking through the handouts*: 'podcast design plan' and 'podcast production plan'.	Students become familiar with the structure and planning process behind the production of a podcast.
Warm-up Stage/Pre-Technology Use **(5 minutes)**	Help students choose a podcast topic that would suit an interview format.	Brainstorm several topics for a podcast based on unit topics (e.g. a movie unit, an interview with a celebrity).	Students brainstorm several ideas for a podcast that they will design and produce, either in pairs or in small groups.

*Available under 'Photocopiable content'.

Main Stage (35 minutes)	Students begin to develop notes for their script.	Help students to work through the handouts to develop their podcast content. Assign a maximum time for the podcast (e.g. 5 or 10 minutes).	Students work through the handouts to develop their podcast design plan, interview questions, and the roles of each student if the task is group work.
Lesson Summation Stage/Post-Technology Activities (5 minutes)	Inform students that they will record their podcast in the next class session.	Tell students that they will record their podcast in the next class session. So, their handouts must be complete and scripts and interview questions ready.	Students will complete the handouts and develop show notes for homework if these have not been completed during class time.

Procedure – Day 3 of 3			
Stage and Timing	Objective	Teacher	Students
Review Stage (5 minutes)	Go over the previous class content (handouts).	Confirm that students have completed their handouts, and are ready to record their podcast with a completed script.	Scripts and show notes should be fully developed, and the podcast production checklist complete.
Warm-up Stage/Pre-Technology Use (10 minutes)	Provide time for students to practice reading their podcasts together.	Check student scripts, show notes, and interview questions Also check that these will meet the previously assigned time limit for the podcast.	Students practice reading their podcasts aloud together.

Main Stage (20 minutes)	Record the podcast.	Assist students in recording the podcast using the appropriate hardware.	Students record their podcast as an MP3, and convert show notes to a PDF.
Lesson Summation Stage/Post-Technology Activities (10 minutes)	Upload podcasts, and show notes to a selected site.	Help students to finalize their content, and upload it to a selected site (such as a class blog).	Students finalize their podcast, and show notes, and upload these to the internet.

Further Considerations	
Follow-Up Activities	Students working in groups can produce several podcasts that can be played back to the class as a 'presentation', with the summary and review worksheets used to keep students focused on listening. These can then be evaluated using rubrics like those given throughout this book.
Contingency Plan(s)	The next lesson in the course syllabus should be ready in case there is a problem at any stage of podcast development. Alternatively, some language games can be prepared to fill in the time if technological problems occur. Several activity sheets for review of previous material should be prepared to allow those students who complete their scripts or recording to keep busy with language content.
Evaluation	What are the biggest frustrations for implementation? Can these be remedied next time? What are the successes of the lesson? What did students get out of this activity? Can more language practice be provided?

Example Implementation:
Podcasting

The Teaching and Learning Context

The example podcast presented here could be used either as a homework task, or used in-class as a short introduction or as a review for listening. Podcasts like this one are designed to be short listening exercises that a teacher may wish to include routinely with a number of episodes created over a school term or year, and specifically to engage students in review. It is suitable for middle school students through to adults who are studying general English, and illustrates the steps required to design and deliver a podcast that could be used with all levels of learners. The associated worksheets, and any related articles or links provided in the show notes can be adapted as needed.

Teaching Material

The teaching material can be broken down into three: the software, the hardware, and the worksheets required to develop and deliver the learning content.

The software

To engage in the production of a podcast, a reliable means of editing, producing, and saving the recordings locally, finding a place to host the recordings, transcripts, and show notes on the internet, and determining a means for distributing the recordings via RSS is essential. A recommendation for teachers who are just starting out with podcasting is to use: Audacity (for editing and recording), Dragon Naturally Speaking (for any necessary transcription), Weebly or WordPress (for hosting show notes, and the podcast files themselves), and FETCHRSS: RSS Generator (to create an RSS feed for the webpage where your files are located). Ultimately, the choice of editing tool, hosting service, and feed creator is yours, and from the many available, you will need to become familiar with the nuances of those that you select.

The hardware

Several hardware items are required to physically record a podcast before it can be edited, distributed, and turned into effective learning content. At a minimum, this would include a device capable of recording audio, and then being able to upload this to a hosting service and create an RSS feed. It is strongly recommended that an external microphone with a pop filter and a quit location be used to perform the recording.

Learning content

A number of worksheets are required in order to smoothly create a podcast for educational purposes. These include one to establish a design plan for the podcast that you intend to produce, which would then allow you to work out the production steps and a potential script that can then be turned into a transcript for inclusion with the show notes. Once the podcast has been recorded, the show notes then need to be developed, along with a complete transcript of the recording. At this stage a worksheet or two can be developed for student use, either in association with listening to the podcast at home for homework or in-class as an introductory or a review exercise undertaken with teacher guidance. The audio file, the transcript, and show notes can then be hosted on the internet, and distributed through RSS.

The worksheets mentioned here have been completed with a sample podcast for use with students, and they include:

- the podcasting design plan
- the podcast production steps
- the podcast transcript
- the podcast show notes
- the podcast student worksheet (one and two)

Procedure

The worksheets provided here are presented as example implementation methods, and are meant to illustrate how a podcast can be planned, produced, transcribed, and then turned into learning content. You can modify this classroom content for use with your students. The worksheets are intended be used in stages, as outlined on the following pages:

Stage one – Development

In the podcast development stage, you will need to focus on the unit and lesson that the podcast may be used for, and on the topic and language points that might be imparted through it. Keeping these aspects in mind, the design plan and the production step worksheets can then be completed. The worksheets that are provided as examples look at accompanying a unit on *'comparing and contrasting'*, and seek to provide familiarity with the expression *'on the other hand ...'*, while using a topic familiar to most students the home.

Stage two – Content creation

After the production and planning stage comes the need to meet with a guest – that is, if the interview mode has been chosen as the most appropriate for the podcast. The show can then be recorded using the questions developed in the scripting section of the production plan, and edited, with music and transitions placed appropriately. A transcript can then be created using voice recognition software, along with show notes. The files can then be hosted, and a distribution feed created. At this point, the language learning content can then be developed, based on the final product, with student worksheets can be created.

Stage three – Student use

The podcast provided could be set for in-class listening at either the beginning or the end of a unit, as it is intended to serve as an introductory or a review piece. Alternatively, it may also be used as a time-filler or be set for homework. The listening portion of the podcast should play for around 5 to 7 minutes when fully produced with music and audio transitions. The associated student worksheets include listening and post-listening tasks, and would take around 30 minutes or so to go over and complete if the podcast is played three times.

Podcast Design Plan	
Podcast Title A new place.	**Group Members** Teacher.
Guest(s) Murray Cod, a student from our school.	
Topic	**Unit/Lesson** Comparing and contrasting
Objectives	1. Identify, become familiar with, and be able to use the expression *'on the other hand'*. 2. Identify and define any unfamiliar expressions or vocabulary (for example, *'got you'*, *'character'*, and *'digs'*).
Planning	**Intent of broadcast** Language practice **Length of broadcast** 5-7 minutes **Number of episodes** 1 **Style of recording** Interview **Recording location** On campus
Producing	**Hardware required** iPad. ☑ **Hardware is operational** ☑ **Hardware is usable** ☑ **Production plan developed***
Publishing	☑ **Files hosted** ☑ **RSS feed created** **Show notes link** www.mycasts.net/snotes001 **Transcript link** www.mycasts/transcript001
Promoting	**Listener involvement** Ask listener's to leave comments/questions; provide links to articles (how to host a housewarming, how to decorate a new place) and any mentioned while recording. **Links spread to** Facebook and school website.

Podcast Production Plan

Introductory Music (30-60 seconds)	"Another word on the board" by The Chalk Dusters.
Introductory Monolog (30-60 seconds)	Welcome back to another episode of the TESOL strategy guide podcast: the place to go for all your language learning needs. I'm your host Noah Tall. Today we will be talking with Murray Cod, a student at our school, and finding out a little about his move into new accommodation.
Topics (3-5 minutes each)	1. A new place, with guest, Murray Cod.
Closing Remarks (up to 2 minutes)	Cheers, Murray. Now, don't forget to check out our show notes, and leave a question or comment to tell us what you think about the show. Catch us next week when one of the school's faculty members is going to drop by and provide some study tips that might help you to ace that next exam. I'm Dr. Noah Tall, and this has been another TESOL strategy guide podcast.
Closing Music (2 minutes)	"Another word on the board" by The Chalk Dusters.

Podcast Transcript

Host: Welcome back to another episode of the TESOL strategy guide podcast: the place to go for all your language learning needs. I'm your host Noah Tall. Today we will be talking with Murray Cod, a student at our school, and finding out a little about his move into new accommodation. So, welcome to the show, Murray. You're a student here at our school, and it's good to talk with you today. Please introduce yourself to our listeners.

Guest: Thank you, sir. Yes, I've been attending this school for over six months now, but I used to find it a little difficult to get to class on time because I lived so far away.

Host: Yes, I'm sure many of our students might find that familiar. I'm guessing that a lot of our students take public transport too. Was it always running late? Is that what made you late to class?

Guest: Sometimes, but I would usually check the 'Klickety-Klack' transport app to find out if the buses were on time or not. So that wasn't really the problem.

Host: I see. We'll put a link to that app in the show notes in case some students here are not familiar with it. So, if the transport isn't so much the problem, then it sounds like maybe a few late nights then?

Guest: Er, maybe. *(Laughs)*

Host: Well, you were up studying of course. No, I got you. Hey, you know this all really leads us into our topic for today. We are going to be talking about your new accommodation. So, it sounds like you have just moved into a new place?

Guest: Indeed, I have. About two weeks ago? Yeah, two weeks ago. I've been living in my new place now for two weeks.

Host: Great. So tell me, what are the main differences between your old place and the new one?

Guest: Probably the biggest difference is that the old place is a lot more modern than the new place.

Host: Okay, so the old place is more modern. On the other hand, the new place has a lot more character, right?

Guest: Well, yes, you could say that. The old place is also lot further away, and it just took way too long to get to school. I didn't like that at all.

Host: That's great to hear. How about the size of the old and new places? Is the new place much bigger?

Guest: Yes, a little bigger, and there are more rooms. I now have a room that I can use just for study.

Host: And the rent?

Guest: Oh, yeah. The rent is a lot cheaper near the school. I will say though, the old place, although more expensive, is more conveniently located to shops. On the other hand, I can now walk to school from the new place so that can save on daily public transport costs.

Host: So, where did you hear about this new place?

Guest: Well, I just spotted a realtor near the west gate bus stop. 'Around Town' Realty is their name, and they had a lot of pretty nice and reasonably priced apartments available near school. It was pretty easy actually.

Host: Yeah, it sounds like it. I'm glad that you're liking your new digs, and we will put a link to that realtor's home page in our show notes – in case anyone else out there is thinking about making a move to a place that's a little closer to school. Also, it seems to be about time to close our episode for today, and say goodbye to listeners for another week. Thank you for dropping by to talk with us, Murray.

Guest: Thank you, and goodbye listeners.

Host: Cheers, Murray. Now, don't forget to check out our show notes, and leave a question or comment to tell us what you think about the show. Catch us next week when one of the school's faculty members is going to drop by and provide some study tips that might help you to ace that next exam. I'm Dr. Noah Tall, and this has been another TESOL strategy guide podcast.

TESOL Strategy Guide Series Podcast Show Notes
Podcast title A new place. **Air date** 03/03/17. **Guest(s)** Murray Cod, a student at our school.
Podcast/Screencast overview We find out about an app that may get you to school on time, meet a new student from our school who talks with us a little about his new place, and find out where to go to rent an apartment near campus.
Episode highlights *We meet Murray Cod, a student at our school.* [00:40] *Murray talks about using the 'Klickety-Klack' app.* [01:33] *Murray starts to compare his old place to his new place.* [02:30] *Murray tells us how he found his new place.* [04:30]

Resources from this episode
    1.   The 'Klickety-Klack' app for Android.
    2.   The 'Klickety-Klack' app for iOS.
    3.   The 'Around Town Realty' home page.

Related articles
    1.   How to host a housewarming.
    2.   How to decorate a new place.

TESOL Strategy Guide Series Podcast
Student Worksheet 1

Instructions

Listen to the latest episode of the TESOL strategy guide podcast.

1. First listening – Listening for the topic

As you listen, try to understand as much as you can and identify the topic.

Q. Which sentence below matches best with the topic of the podcast:

☐ The podcast is about public transport.

☐ The podcast is about comparing a new place to an old one.

☐ The podcast is about study tips to help you ace an exam.

2. Second listening – Listening for detail

As you listen, try to catch as many details as you can, and place a tick (✓) in the correct column.

Which place …	New Place	Old Place
is more modern?		
is bigger?		
has higher rent?		
has more rooms?		
is closer to school?		

(Use with Worksheet Two)

TESOL Strategy Guide Series Podcast
Student Worksheet 2

3. Third listening – Listening for expressions and vocabulary

As you listen, pay close attention to any words or phrases that may be new to you. Try to write down as many as you can, and then try to decide what they might mean.

New word/expression	Possible meaning
1.	
2.	
3.	
4.	
5.	
6.	

4. After listening – What about you?

Now think about where you live. What things are important or not important to you? Tick (✓) the appropriate column.

My place ...	Important	Not Important
is modern		
is big		
has low rent		
has many rooms		
is close to school/work		
is near to shops		
is near public transport		

(Use with Worksheet One)

Lesson Plan Guide for Screencasting	
Teaching Context	
Level of Proficiency and Maturity	Beginner to advanced. Adaptable for use with young learners through to adults.
Lesson Length	Suitable for several lessons over a week. Homework completion components. Time allotted for each class: 50 minutes.
Lesson Topic	Variable. Anything suited to a demonstration, procedure, or tutorial would work well (e.g. how to create a glog using Glogster).
Objectives	1. Enhance communication skills through collaborative learning, demonstrations, and script development. 2. Strengthen multiple literacies (computer literacy, digital literacy, and English literacy).
Outcomes	1. Students identify significant points on a topic, and use these in a tutorial. 2. Transfer current knowledge into learning and the use and understanding of technological systems.
Relevant Prior Learning	None required. Podcasting or digital storytelling experience helpful.

Teacher Preparation	
Hardware	Computer or tablet with audio recording capability (e.g. built-in or external microphone). USB sticks or Google Drive for storage.
Software	Screencasting software (e.g. Screencast-O-Matic)
Webpage Links	Screencast-O-Matic screencast.com
Additional Resources	Handouts*: • Screencast summary and review • Screencast design plan • Screencasting production plan • Screencast show notes

*Available under 'Photocopiable content'.

Procedure – Day 1 of 3			
Stage and Timing	Objective	Teacher	Students
Introductory Stage (5 minutes)	Determine student familiarity with screencasts, and find out what tutorial type videos students have watched.	Determine student familiarity with screencasts by introducing examples (e.g. from Screencast.com or YouTube).	Express opinions about the video tutorials they have used in the past.
Warm-up Stage/Pre-Technology Use (5 minutes)	Brainstorm good topics for screencasts, provide links to examples of suitable tutorial type screencasts.	Help students to think of topics that they can later use to make their own screencasts, and provide links to suitable examples.	Students start to think about the topics suitable for screencasts, and are introduced to some screencasts that they can watch later.

Main Stage (20 minutes)	Play a tutorial type podcast to students, that is suitable to their language level.	Play a short screencast to students, at a maximum of three times, and have them complete the 'Screencast Summary and Review' handout*.	Students will watch the screencast, and complete the associated handout.
Lesson Summation Stage/Post-Technology Activities (10 minutes)	Go through the worksheet answers with students, and remind them of screencasts that are suitable for language learning.	Go over the worksheet with students, and check their answers. Finish the lesson by providing several links for students to watch in their own time.	Students are called on to provide their answers from the worksheet, and are provided with suitable screencast links that they can use to improve their English.

*Available under 'Photocopiable content'.

Procedure – Day 2 of 3			
Stage and Timing	**Objective**	**Teacher**	**Students**
Review Stage **(5 minutes)**	Remind students of screencasts, the types of screencast, and the structure of a screencast.	Introduce the structure of screencasts by talking through the handouts*: 'screencast design plan' and 'screencast production plan'.	Students become familiar with the structure and planning process behind the production of a screencast.
Warm-up Stage/Pre-Technology Use **(5 minutes)**	Help students choose a screencast topic that would suit a tutorial format.	Brainstorm several topics for a screencast that is based on unit topics (e.g. demonstration speech unit, how to make a glog on Glogster).	Students brainstorm several ideas for a screencast that they will design and produce in pairs or in small groups.

*Available under 'Photocopiable content'.

Main Stage (35 minutes)	Students begin to develop notes for their script.	Help students to work through the handouts to develop their screencast content. Assign a maximum time for the screencast (e.g. 5 or 10 minutes).	Students work through the handouts to develop their screencast design plan, script, and the roles of each student if the task is group work.
Lesson Summation Stage/Post-Technology Activities (5 minutes)	Inform students that they will record their screencast in the next class session. This will require all students have access to a computer or a device to allow for this to occur.	Tell students that they will record their screencast in the next class session. This means that their handouts must be complete and their scripts are ready.	Students will complete the handouts and develop program notes for homework if these have not been completed during class time.

Procedure – Day 3 of 3			
Stage and Timing	**Objective**	**Teacher**	**Students**
Review Stage **(5 minutes)**	Go over the previous class content (handouts).	Confirm that students have completed their handouts, and are ready to record their screencast with a completed script.	Scripts and program notes should be fully developed, and the screencast production checklist complete.
Warm-up Stage/Pre-Technology Use **(10 minutes)**	Provide time for students to practice reading their screencasts together.	Check student scripts, show notes, and interview questions. Also check that these will meet the previously assigned time limit for the screencast.	Students practice reading their screencasts aloud together.

Main Stage (20 minutes)	Record the screencast.	Assist students in recording the screencast using the appropriate software.	Students record their screencast as an MP4, and convert program notes to a PDF.
Lesson Summation Stage/Post-Technology Activities (10 minutes)	Upload screencasts and program notes to a selected site.	Help students to finalize their content, and upload it to a selected site (such as a class blog, or YouTube).	Students finalize their screencast and program notes, and upload these to the internet.

Further Considerations	
Follow-Up Activities	Students working in groups can produce several screencasts that can be played back to the class as a kind of presentation, using the summary and review worksheets to keep the other students focused. These can then be evaluated using rubrics like those found throughout this book. Students can be assigned homework, and work as pairs, to make screencast vocabulary flashcards as a way to review important vocabulary.
Contingency Plan(s)	The next lesson in the course syllabus should be ready in case there is a problem at any stage of screencast development. Alternatively, some language games can be prepared to fill in the time if technological problems occur. Several activity sheets for review of previous material should be prepared to allow those students who complete their scripts or recording to keep busy with language content.
Evaluation	What are the biggest frustrations for implementation? Can these be remedied next time? What are the successes of the lesson? What did students get out of this activity? Can more language practice be provided?

Example Implementation:
Screencasting

The Teaching and Learning Context

The example of screencast use here could be applied by any teacher when grading a student's homework. The method of implementation would be well suited for any school, subject, or grade-level of students. Its suitability for use with second-language learners is dependent only on the teacher's ability to adapt the use of their language to suit the level of their learners as they conduct the screencast. If you are using this model with your students to deliver feedback on writing, or adapting it work with other kinds of electronic submissions, then you would need to adapt your language use based on your knowledge of the students.

Descriptive Feedback

Descriptive feedback should be designed to help learners adjust what they are doing so that they can improve (Davies, 2007), and it should therefore help students identify what they are doing well, what areas they might need to cultivate, and what steps they may be able to take to develop themselves. The feedback should be clear, specific, meaningful, and timely.

It is important to consider several factors when conducting descriptive feedback, including the timing of when it is provided, the amount, the way it is provided, and who it is going to be provided to.

Timing
Provide feedback as often as possible: immediately for something that is right or wrong; later if a comprehensive review is needed (but not too long so that it would not make a difference).

Amount
Prioritize the most important points for feedback. Select points that are reflective of learning goals. Consider student level when grading.

Mode

Immediate feedback may be best in person, or in passing students on a classroom walk-around.

Interactive feedback, talking directly with one student at a time, may be best for feedback on spoken tasks.

Written feedback may be best on written work.

Demonstrations could be required to ensure students know how to perform a task.

Audience

Individual feedback may see students respond by thinking "the teacher values me".

Group/whole-class feedback may be best when all or most students require the same feedback: good or bad (for example, praise on completing a task effectively, or a language point that all students need consistent correction on).

Descriptive Feedback Model for Screencasting

Providing a screencast while conducting descriptive grading of student submissions is perhaps one of the best ways to incorporate the use of screencasting in your classes. This is because you will be able to perform the integration of technology and screencast use without much additional time allotted to carrying out the task. It will also provide second-language learners with additional language practice, as you model good work for them, as well as allowing them to establish a more personal connection with you as their teacher.

Teaching Material

The teaching material required can be broken down into three: the software, the hardware, and the student work that requires grading.

The software

Any screencasting software can be used for providing feedback on student produced digital content. One option might be Screen-O-Matic as it can be used browser-based or installed locally.

The hardware

The minimum hardware required is a device that can run the software that you have chosen to use for screencasting, and has either a built-in microphone or a means to connect an external microphone (one with a pop filter). You could also need a scanner if seeking to screencast non-digitized content.

Learning content

The learning content in this context is any student-produced content that can be graded. The content can be either already in a digital format, and returned in digital form with feedback, or it can be digitalized.

Procedure

The type of content that is being graded will reflect on how you annotate the material and dictate feedback. For example, if you are using Microsoft Word files, then you will be able to use features such as 'Track changes' along with notes, and explain why these are being changed or added as you screencast. Other options are using a 'Note' program to add sticky notes to content as you grade or keep a rolling list of comments. You may also simply use the mouse as a pointer to highlight areas of focus, and provide spoken feedback regarding any points of note. In any of these cases, all of the steps below are similar, and they are suitable to follow for the screencasting of descriptive feedback of any student-produced content.

Step one – Identify
Identify the type of assignment or work that you will conduct your descriptive feedback on (for example, blog post, digital story, essay, glog poster, or slideshow presentation).

Step two – Select
Select the application to conduct the screencast, and open student work that is ready for grading.

Step three - Grade
Grade your students' work as you normally would, and during the time that is normally allotted for conducting such a task, except dictate feedback as you annotate and highlight the aspects of students' work that needs correcting, praising, or improving. Working with content that has not yet been digitialized may require the scanning of student worksheets into a single PDF, and then developing a

screencast that goes through this file while grading, annotating, and dictating. Alternatively, a web camera could be used that captures the hardcopy content physically being graded along with the teacher comments, so that annotations could be made directly onto students' work, and then returned to them.

Step four – Distribute

Save and upload the screencast as a single file for each student, or as a single file containing all of the students' feedback. In either case, it would then be available for each student and stakeholder, as well as a whole-class review when required.

14
Photocopiable material

This section of the book contains all the photocopiable handouts, and you can feel free to make as many copies as you require for teaching purposes and for use within your classes. Any other use or distribution should include a citation to the source of the content.

There are a number of podcasts and screencasts available on the internet from sites like YouTube. For a teacher to use these in class would require prescreening to ensure that they are appropriate for students to listen to or view, and to determine if they are suitable for a particular classroom objective or specific standards. It may therefore be necessary for you to develop your own podcast or screencast, and a planning guide and production step checklist is essential for this. Providing students with handouts to use during the planning and production stages of podcast and screencast creation will also help to guide them in their development, and examples for each have been provided here. The following planning guides and production steps can be used by a teacher to create a podcast or screencast for their classes, and by students to develop their own podcasts and screencasts for particular learning objectives.

When using screencasts with students, it is important to check that they understand the content that is being presented to them at the surface level and at the deep level. One way of doing this is to have them make notes as they watch a screencast, and then convert these notes into a paragraph using sentence prompts; in this way, they can make meaning out of what they are learning and develop their own understanding of the screencast. More specific points regarding knowledge related to the content presented can be determined by asking questions specifically on that content in order to have students reproduce any information that they were presented with, and is of relevance to their continued learning and course participation. To this end, the 'screencast summary and review handout resource notes' and the 'screencast summary and review handout' are provided. If needed, additional questions or points of summary can be added as required.

Also provided is a lesson plan template that can be used for considering how best to integrate the steps for using podcasts and screencasts with your classes. It is meant to act as means to begin thinking about how to implement aspects of what has been discovered through this book with your classes, and it should be supplemented with any necessary material. The staging as well as other aspects of the lesson should be adjusted as required.

The following photocopiable material is available:

- Podcast design plan resource notes
- Podcast design plan handout
- Podcast production plan resource notes
- Podcast production plan handout
- Screencast design plan resource notes
- Screencast design plan handout
- Screencast production plan resource notes
- Screencast production plan handout
- Podcast/Screencast summary and review resource notes
- Podcast/Screencast summary and review handout
- Podcast/Screencast show/program notes resource notes
- Podcast/Screencast show/program notes handout
- Lesson plan template

Podcast Design Plan
Resource Notes

Podcast Title A title is chosen by students, and written here.	**Group Members** Student names are listed here.

Guest(s) Potential guest(s) selected, and name(s) written here.

Topic	What unit or lesson will be the focus?
Objectives	List the learning or interview objectives here.
Planning	What is the intent of the broadcast? How long will it go for? Will there be one long episode, or a series of shorter episodes? What style will the recording take? (e.g. audio or video) Where will the recording take place?
Producing	Appropriate hardware is required (e.g. microphone, webcam). Ensure that hardware is working, and students know how to use it. A production plan will need to be developed.
Publishing	Create an RSS feed to distribute your podcast, and provide access to show notes for listeners.
Promoting	Attempt to involve listeners: ask questions that will lead to comments being left (e.g. ask for future topic suggestions, or ask for questions to be left for you to answer in another episode); spread links to the episode; show notes or behind-the-scenes photos across social media.

Podcast Design Plan Handout	
Podcast Title	**Group Members**
Guest(s) _____	

Topic	Unit/Lesson _____
Objectives	1. _____ 2. _____
Planning	Intent of broadcast _____ Length of broadcast _____ Number of episodes _____ Style of recording _____ Recording location _____
Producing	Hardware required _____ _____ ☐ Hardware is operational ☐ Hardware is usable ☐ Production plan developed*
Publishing	☐ Files hosted ☐ RSS Feed created Show notes link _____ Transcript link _____
Promoting	Listener involvement _____ Links spread to _____

*Use the 'Podcast Production Plan Handout'.

Podcast Production Plan Resource Notes	
Introductory Music (30-60 seconds)	Play a unique identifier for your show that audience members can associate with you. This can then lead into the podcast, with the introduction monolog then spoken as a voiceover.
Introductory Monolog (30-60 seconds)	State who you are, introduce any guests, and state the topics to be discussed.
Topics (3-5 minutes each)	Stay focused on the key aspects of the topic by asking guests specific questions (or posing questions to yourself), and guiding guests back on track where necessary. It is advisable to prepare a script to follow for solo podcasts. Throughout each topic, remind the listeners that any resources or links will be posted as show notes, and where these can be obtained.
Closing Remarks (up to 2 minutes)	Thank the audience for listening, thank any guests, mention the topic and/or guests of the next show, and remind the audience where to go for show notes.
Closing Music (2 minutes)	Play out the podcast with the same music as used in the introduction. This can be started during the closing remarks and continue afterwards.

Podcast Production Plan Handout	
Introductory Music (30-60 seconds)	
Introductory Monolog (30-60 seconds)	
Topics (3-5 minutes each)	
Closing Remarks (up to 2 minutes)	
Closing Music (2 minutes)	

Screencast Design Plan Resource Notes	
Screencast Title A title is chosen by students, and written here.	**Group Members** Student names are listed here.
Application(s) Name the application(s) taking focus here.	
Topic	What unit or lesson will be covered?
Objectives	List the learning objectives of the screencast.
Format	Determine the format based on lesson objectives (e.g. demonstration, presentation, tutorial).
Scripting	Walk through the steps on screen that you intend to discuss; prepare an outline or script as you go. Read through the script for practice, and to determine the time required for recording.
Capturing	Decide on the area of the screen, or the applications, to be recorded. Recording can be conducted simultaneously with narration, or the voiceover can be added in postproduction.
Editing	Edit out mistakes; trim, add or sync the narration; add call-outs, zooms, and annotations.
Publishing	Publish the movie to a YouTube channel, learner management system (LMS), or distribute for in-class delivery. Provide access to program notes.
Promoting and Engaging	Promote the screencast on the class website for various stakeholders to see, and engage viewers by asking questions or asking them to comment.

Screencast Design Plan Handout	
Screencast Title	**Group Members**

Application(s) _____

Topic	Unit/Lesson _____
Objectives	1. _____
	2. _____
Format	Type _____
Scripting	Time required _____
	☐ Production plan developed*
Capturing	Area(s)/applications recorded _____
	_____
	Hardware required _____
	_____
	☐ Hardware is operational
	☐ Hardware is usable
Editing	☐ Narration synced
	☐ Annotations, callouts, and zooms applied
Publishing	Screencast link _____
	Program notes link _____
	Transcript link _____
Promoting and Engaging	Links spread to _____
	_____
	Viewer involvement _____
	_____

*Use the 'Screencast Production Plan Handout'.

Screencast Production Plan Resource Notes	
Introduction (30-60 seconds)	Select the screen area that will become the focus, and provide a voiceover introduction to the topic or topics that will be discussed, with an overview of the steps involved.
Topics (3-5 minutes each)	Each topic-based section needs to stay on script Keep the viewer informed, and tell them everything that you are doing. Zoom into and highlight features only when they are being discussed. Use annotations and callouts where necessary, and edit out any pauses or mistakes in post-production.
Closing Remarks (up to 2 minutes)	Finish off by thanking the viewers and remind them of the topics covered and the knowledge and skills that have been imparted by watching the screencast, and how these skills can now be put to use.

Screencast Production Plan Handout	
Introduction **(30-60 seconds)**	
Topics **(3-5 minutes** **each)**	
Closing Remarks **(up to 2 minutes)**	

Podcast/Screencast Summary and Review Resource Notes

Podcast/Screencast Title	Group Members
A title is chosen by students, and written here.	Student names are listed here.

Summary Use sentence prompts to stimulate deep learning.

I learned Students identify and write at least one thing new that they learned from the podcast/screencast.

In particular I learned Students identify and write something new they learned that was surprising to them.

I really understood Students identify and write something new that they learned and understood very well.

I didn't really understand Students write something that they did not understand at all or need further clarification on.

This podcast/screencast has helped me better understand Students identify and write the objective of the screencast.

Review Questions (Use *Wh*-type questions to help promote surface learning – What? When? Where? Why? How?).

1. What … ? _____

_____

2. When … ? _____

_____

3. Where … ? _____

_____

4. Why … ? _____

_____

Podcast/Screencast Summary and Review Handout

Podcast/Screencast Title	Group Members

Summary

I learned _____

_____

In particular I learned _____

_____

I really understood _____

_____

I didn't really understand _____

_____

This podcast/screencast has helped me better understand ___

_____

Review Questions

1. _____

_____

2. _____

_____

3. _____

_____

4. _____

_____

Podcast/Screencast Show/Program Notes
Resource Notes

Group members Write the name of group members here.

Image Provide an image representative of your podcast, or an image of the guests interviewed (for podcasts) or an image representative of the application discussed (for screencasts).

Podcast/Screencast title Write its name here.

Air date Write the date of the broadcast here.

Guest(s) Write the name(s) of guests here.

Podcast/Screencast overview

Provide a short reminder of the topic of the podcast/screencast.

Podcasts – reminder of guest credentials, or your own if there were no guests.

Screencasts – reminder of the importance of the applications(s) discussed.

Episode highlights

Provide topic highlights using a hook, along with the time the topic is discussed. For example: *Dr. Kent's tips to pass the TOEIC, and how you can master the exam easily.* [03:10]

Resources from this episode

Provide links to all resources mentioned, and anything that you suggested as beneficial for viewers or listeners to follow up on. This might include: internet pages, journal articles, or any books, TV shows, and commercial products recommended.

Related articles

Include links to places such as: an article (online or offline), a blog post, or a wiki page.

Podcast/Screencast Show/Program Notes
Handout

Group members _____

> **Image**

Podcast/Screencast title _____

Air date _____

Guest(s) _____

Podcast/Screencast overview

_____
_____
_____

Episode highlights

_____
_____
_____
_____
_____

Resources from this episode

_____
_____
_____

Related articles

_____
_____
_____

Lesson Plan Template

Teaching Context

Level of Proficiency and Maturity	
Lesson Length	
Lesson Topic	
Objectives	
Outcomes	
Relevant Prior Learning	

Teacher Preparation

Hardware	
Software	
Webpage Links	
Additional Resources	

Procedure			
Stage and Timing	Objective	Teacher	Students
Review Stage (if required)			
Warm-up Stage/Pre-Technology Use			
Main Stage/ Technology-based Activity			
Practice Stage			
Lesson Summation Stage/Post-Technology Activities			

Further Considerations	
Follow-Up Activities	
Contingency Plan(s)	
Evaluation	

15

Resources list

As sites continuously go down, merge, and emerge, perhaps only a small selection of all appropriate resource content should be presented here. An attempt at keeping the number of resources to a select few for each type also provides a sample that is both comprehensive and extensive, but not overwhelming. Like any other instructor resource list, individuals will be able to add to the content as they find material that is useful, creating their own bookmark list, and over time, come to curate a vast resource library tailored to their individual teaching and learning context. Each section of this list is broken down into applications that are mostly all freely available for use with Android or iOS devices, computers, or web-based platforms.

Teachers who wish to make notes, or to record any additional resources that they come across, can use the notes section at the end of this chapter.

The following content is covered:

- App creation
- Audio creation/editing
- Blogs
- Bookmarking
- Books
- Coding
- Comic strip generators
- Copyright
- Digital story creation
- Image resources
- Image editing
- Interactive whiteboards
- Mashups
- Media timelines
- Music resources
- Podcasting
- Podcatchers
- Presentations
- Publishing
- QR codes
- Rubrics
- Screencasting
- Storyboarding and scripting
- Story creation apps
- Video editing
- Video resources
- WebQuests
- Wikis

App Creation

Android – n/a

iOS – n/a

Computer – n/a

Web

Android Creator [free/paid] creates free Android apps without the need for programming knowledge.

AppMakr [free/paid] is a template based application creator that relies on drag and drop of elements for the development of no-coding required applications. It is available in a variety of languages.

Appy Pie [free/paid] relies on templates as well as drag and drop for users to begin creating their app. It requires no coding skills.

AppYourself [paid] is an app creation tool aimed at the business market.

Como DIY [paid] is a do-it-yourself app creation tool aimed to mostly target to businesses, and is available in a number of languages.

iBuildApp [paid] is a template driven app creator for iPhone and Android phones.

Audio Creation/Editing

Android

> *PCM Recorder* [free] is a simple voice recorder.
>
> *Pocket WavePad* [free] records edits and adds effects to audio.
>
> *TapeMachine* [paid] is a graphical sound recorder and editor.

iOS

> *Pocket WavePad* [free] records edits and adds effects to audio.
>
> *Voice Memos* [paid] is voice recorder that allows multitasking.

Computer

> *Audacity* [free] is an open source digital editing program available for Mac and PC which you can use to record, edit and mix narration and music.
>
> *Pocket WavePad* [free] records, edits, and adds effects to audio for Mac.

GoldWave [free/paid] is a digital audio editor that provides simple recording as well as more sophisticated processing, restoration, enhancement, and conversion for Windows and Linux. A free version is available for evaluation purposes, after which a lifetime license can be purchased.

Web

Twistedwave [free] is a browser-based audio editor that can record or edit any audio file.

Blogs

Android

Blogaway [free] is a simple application to allow blogging on-the-go. It works with Blogger and allows for post creation, adding of photos, videos, multiple account management, saving of drafts, bookmarking, and a host of formatting options.

iOS

Disqus [free] is a commenting system that can be included in blogs as an add-on. The application provides an easy way to moderate comments and publish responses to keep engagement levels high.

TravelPod – Travel Blog [free] is a blogging application that works on- and offline, and is designed to be used while traveling.

Computer – n/a

Web

Blogger.com [free] will host your blog for free, and aside from being very easy to use, it allows some level of privacy so it can be suitable for use as a class blogging site. From a single account, you can create as many blogs as you wish and determine who is allowed to comment on the content.

BuzzSumo [paid] allows users to search for blog posts that have been highly shared across social media.

Edublogs.org [free] allows teachers to create and mange their own and students' websites. There is room for customization of design and the ability to add various media to this private and secure platform.

Kidblog.org [free] is an easy-to-use, safe, and secure publishing platform designed for students in grades K-12. There are a number of excellent features including privacy and password protection, and there is no need for student personal information to be collected, nor is there any advertising. It is free for up to fifty students per class.

WordPress.org [free] is one of the most popular blogging platforms in use today as it is open-source and is easily customizable. The downloadable software for self-hosting purposes is much more flexible than that available on the blogging platform.

Twitter [free] deserves a mention here as it is useful for microblogging (posting short frequent updates). It allows users to post and read short 140-character posts called 'tweets'.

Tumblr [free] is a blogging platform open to those over thirteen years of age, with most users using pen names over their real names when blogging. Users can post on their blog, follow others, and search posts. It is unique in that posts are divided into media types: text, photo, quote, link, chat, audio, and video.

Bookmarking

Android

Bookmark [free] is a cross-platform app that allows for the syncing of bookmarks across different browsers and devices.

Delicious [free] provides users with the ability to organize links to content on the internet that they would like to save, the ability to discover links, edit tags and comments, and also to explore content saved by friends.

Facebook Save [free] is a built-in option for saving Facebook news content to read at a later date.

Instapaper [free] provides an offline archiving solution for web pages, and it presents this content to be read in newspaper fashion. Content can be highlighted, and notes can be added while reading.

Pinterest [free] allows users to pin posts (for example, web pages, images, and videos) and organize them around a common theme.

Pocket [free] integrates with a large number of third party applications that allow for the building of bookmarks. Web pages, videos, images, and whatever else can be used offline for bookmarking. Archiving maintains the links but removes the content from offline availability.

iOS

Delicious [free] allows users to save content from the internet (including web pages, blog posts, tweets, pictures, and video), and provides options for searching through others' collections of links.

Facebook Save [free] is a built-in option for saving Facebook news content to read at a later date.

Instapaper [free] provides an offline archiving solution for web pages and presents this content to be read in newspaper fashion. Content can be highlighted, and notes can be added while reading.

Pinterest [free] allows users to pin posts (for example, web pages, images, and videos) and organize them around a common theme.

Pocket [free] integrates with a large number of third party applications that allow for the building of bookmarks. Web pages, videos, images, and whatever else can be used offline for bookmarking. Archiving maintains the links but removes the content from offline availability.

Computer

EdwinSoft's UltimateDemon [paid] is link building software that helps to provide search engine optimization to a website.

Pinterest [free] allows users to pin posts (for example, web pages, images, and videos) and organize them around a common theme.

Pocket [free] integrates with a large number of third party applications that allow for the building of bookmarks. Web pages, videos, images, and whatever else can be used offline for bookmarking. Archiving maintains the links but removes the content from offline availability.

ReadKit [trial/paid] offers an Apple Mac curative and archiving platform for the content found in your other bookmarking applications (like Pocket and Instapaper) and RSS readers, and provides an extra level of organization to this content.

Web

Delicious [free] is a social bookmarking site that allows users to bookmark webpages to the internet instead of locally.

Facebook Save [free] is a built-in option for saving Facebook news content to read at a later date.

Instapaper [free] provides an offline archiving solution for web pages, and it presents this content to be read in newspaper fashion. Content can be highlighted, and notes can be added while reading.

OnlyWire [paid] works with WordPress and offers automatic submission of content to social networking and social bookmarking sites.

Pocket [free] integrates with a large number of third party applications that allow for the building of bookmarks. Web pages, videos, images, and whatever else can be used offline for bookmarking. Archiving maintains the links but removes the content from offline availability.

Books

Android

Wattpad Free Books [free] provides access to free stories and books written by aspiring authors.

iOS

Free Books – Ultimate Classics Library [free] features free access to 23,469 classic books.

Computer – n/a

Web

BookRix [free] allows access to thousands of books to read either online or to download as ebooks.

Children's Storybooks Online [free] provides a series of illustrated stories for all ages to read.

Coding

Android

Run Marco! [free] offers users the opportunity to play an adventure game while they learn to code. The application presents instructions using 'Blocky', which is the same as that used by the official Hour of Code tutorials.

Tynker [free] is an easy way for children to learn programming skills as they solve puzzles to learn concepts and build games, or control robots and drones. A number of templates are available for free.

iOS

Codea [paid] is a software development tool that uses the Lua programming language to teach users how to program.

Hopscotch [free] is an application that allows users to begin learning to code by making games similar to Angry Birds, and sharing them so others can play them.

ScratchJr [free] allows users to program their own interactive stories and games by snapping together graphical programming blocks. The application was inspired by the Scratch programming language.

Tynker [free] is an easy way for children to learn programming skills as they solve puzzles to learn concepts and build games, or control robots and drones. A number of templates are available for free.

Computer

Scratch [free] allows users to create stories, games, and animations using the Scratch programming language, and then share these with others. It is a project of the Lifelong Kindergarten Group at the MIT Media Lab.

Lightbot – Programming Puzzles [paid] is an OS X game-based application that allows players to use programming logic to solve levels. The app is also available for Android and iOS devices.

Web – n/a

Comic Strip Generators

Android

Comic Maker [free] creates comics from the photo gallery.

Comic Strip It! Lite [free] takes photos or use photo gallery images to create a comic.

iOS

Comic Life 3 [paid] turns photos into comic pages, or creates an entire comic from scratch using templates to build pages with speech balloons, comic lettering, and photo filters.

ToonTastic [free] is a wizard-based animated comic or cartoon creator.

Strip Designer [paid] is software for comic creation that uses camera, library, or Facebook photo options to create a comic.

Computer

Comic Creator [paid] is a basic template driven comic creator for use on a Windows computer.

Web

Pixton [free/paid] is an easy to use comprehensive online comic creator that supports narration, and offers a range of signup options from a free fun option to paid educator/business accounts.

MakeBeliefsComix [free] is a basic comic creator that uses black and white images over a four-panel comic strip. An iOS version is also available.

Toonlet [free] allows for anyone to create their own cartoon characters and web comics.

Toondoo [free] allows for the drag and drop creation of comic strips. An iOS version is also available.

Copyright

Android – n/a

iOS – n/a

Computer – n/a

Web

Creative Commons Licenses [free] gives detailed information regarding the various types of licensing afforded to creative commons, and the permissions that each license grants for the use specific works.

Image Codr [free] can assist learners and teachers alike in determining how a Flickr image can be used (as determined by the original photographer), and provides users with an automatically generated Creative Commons citation regarding the images use within digital projects.

Digital Story Creation

Android

Com-Phone Story Maker [free] combines audio, photos, and text to create stories while allowing for three different layers of audio.

WeVideo [free] is a web-based video editor that can mix images, text, video, and audio.

iOS

30hands [free] creates a story by adding narration to photos.

Magisto [free] uses a wizard to create a short video based on provided images or video content.

Splice [free/paid] combines photos, videos, music and narrations. Effects and transitions can be added.

WeVideo [free] is a web-based video editor that can mix images, text, video, and audio.

Computer

iMovie [paid] provides video creation and editing software that can create easily shareable content on a Mac. An iOS version is available.

Microsoft Photo Story 3 [free] for Windows lets you create slideshows from a wizard that includes audio, narration, and images.

Windows Movie Maker [free] for Windows operating systems is a video editing software application that allows for narration, audio, images, and video to be mixed and edited, and it comes with transitions and special effects.

Web

Animoto [paid] allows users to submit songs, choose a theme, add their photos, videos, and text to create a digital story that they can share.

Meograph [free] is a digital storytelling tool that relies on Google Earth to create map-based and timeline-based narrated stories.

WeVideo [free] is a web-based video editor that can mix images, text, video, and audio.

Image Resources

Android – n/a

iOS – n/a

Computer – n/a

Web

Cagle Cartoons [free] provides access to a number of political cartoons from around the world. The images are organized by topic with artists categorized by country.

Flickr Creative Commons [free] provides images that can be used for almost any educational project, as long as proper citation is followed

FreeFoto.com [free] has a photos area that is available under three licensing options: recognition, Creative Commons, and commercial.

Morguefile [free] provides a range of images that are copyright free, and are available for use with few or no restrictions.

Pics4Learning.com [free] is a website that provides safe and free images for educational uses. Images here are copyright-friendly and can be used for classrooms, multimedia projects, websites, videos, portfolios, or other projects.

PicSearch [free] allows you to search the internet for images, but be aware that the image may not be copyright-free, or that it may require permission to be used in projects or in any other educational contexts.

The Library of Congress Prints & Photographs Online Catalog [free] makes an attempt to ensure that as many of their images as possible are available online in a digital format.

Wikimedia [free] serves as a point from where all the images and video posted in Wikipedia can be viewed. Most of the images found here are either copyright-free or free for use with minimal restrictions.

Image Editing

Android

PicSay [free] can edit photos, overlay titles, and add special effects.

FX Camera [free] is a photo booth app that allows users to add various effects to photographs.

iOS

PhotoPad [free] can create, edit, and save vector illustrations. It can also work with photo library images.

ScreenChomp [free] allows you to share, explain, and markup images.

Computer

PhotoPad [paid] is an image editor for OS X.

PaintShop Pro [paid] is a comprehensive image editing package for Windows.

Web

Adobe Photoshop CC [paid] is a comprehensive cloud-based image editing package.

Phixr [free] is an online photo editor with various filters and effects, and it can connect to various social media sites.

FotoFlexer [free] is an online image editor offering a number of effects, distortions, and other features.

Pixlr [paid] is a comprehensive online photo editing app.

Interactive Whiteboards

Android

ExplainEverything [free] allows users to share their content by using an interactive screencasting whiteboard.

Interactive Whiteboard [free] is a virtual whiteboard that can be used for drawing or teaching various concepts as it allows for multiple finger input, straight line drawing mode, drawing move mode, and various other features.

PPT and Whiteboard Sharing [free] provides a way to share presentations, videos, and drawings in various settings including the classroom, the boardroom, and online meetings.

Whiteboard: Collaborative Draw [free] is a collaborative drawing application that allows real-time painting.

iOS

Doceri [trial/paid] combines screencasting, desktop control, and an interactive whiteboard in one application, with control through Airplay or through Mac or PC.

Educreations Interactive Whiteboard [free] is an interactive whiteboard and screencasting tool that allows annotation, animation, and narration of a number of content types.

Screenchomp [free] allows users to annotate pictures or to use the application as a whiteboard. Any work completed with the application can be saved automatically to the internet.

ShowMe Interactive Whiteboard [free] allows voice-over recording of whiteboard interactions so that tutorials can be created easily before being shared online.

Computer

Open Sakore [free] is open-source and it is dedicated to teacher and student use. It allows for insertion of multiple document types, along with annotation capabilities for commenting drawing and highlighting content.

Smoothboard Air [free] is a collaborative interactive whiteboard for multiple iPads and for Android tablets. It allows users to annotate desktop applications wirelessly through the use of a web browser.

Web

A Web Whiteboard [free] is a online whiteboard application that allows a number of devices (like computers, tablets, and smartphones), to draw sketches, and to collaborate with others around the globe.

Realtime Board [free] is a whiteboard in a browser that allows for collaboration among a number of users.

Twiddla [free] is a web-based meeting environment that allows users to mark up photos, graphics, and websites, or to just start out with a blank canvas.

Web Whiteboard [free] is a simple way to draw and write together online by creating an online whiteboard with a click, and sharing it live or by sending the link to others.

Mashups

Android

    Edjing 5 DJ Music Mixer [free] not only transforms any android device into a turntable, but it provides access to a range of music libraries.

iOS

    iMashup [paid] is a professional quality remixing app that allows users to create their own mashups and remixes.

    Pacemaker [free] allows users to create and save mixes on an iPhone or iWatch, and to DJ live from iPad devices.

Computer

    Mixxx [free] is an advanced open source DJ package that includes an extensive array of features for OS X and Windows.

Web

    Mashstix [free] is a website with user submitted mashups available.

Media Timelines

Android

RWT Timelines [free] allows students to create a graphical representation of any event or process by displaying items sequentially along a line. The final product can be exported as a pdf, or saved to the device's camera roll.

Timeline [free] allows users to create timelines and associate them with colors, and to view multiple timelines together. It is a useful reference tool for remembering dates.

iOS

TimelineBuilder [paid] allows users to create custom timelines with images and text with unique beginning and end dates.

Timeline Maker [free] provides an easy way to display a series of events in a chronological order.

Computer

Edraw Timeline Maker [paid] is a tool that makes it simple to create a professional looking timeline, history, schedule, time table, or project plan diagram from scratch.

TimelineMaker [paid] provides a simplified timeline charting tool aimed at project planners, and business professionals, and those in educational contexts.

Web

Capzles [free] allows users to create rich multimedia experiences from videos, photos, music, blogs, and documents by integrating these into a timeline of sequential events, and then share them on various social media platforms.

Hstry [free] is specifically designed for the education sector, and it allows teachers and students to create interactive timelines for assignments and online sharing.

OurStory [free] offers a means for creating story-based timelines with pictures.

Timeline [free] from *readwritethink* allows students of all ages to easily create a graphical representation of related items or events in sequential order and display them along a line using various images and text.

TimeGlider [free] is a web-based timeline project creator that allows zooming and panning across timelines. Users are able to set the size of events as they relate to importance.

Tiki-Toki [free/paid] is a web-based timeline editor that allows viewing of timelines in 3D, and it allows for the integration of images and videos.

WhenInTime [free] is a web application for creating and sharing media-based timelines.

Music Resources

Android

FindSounds [free] can be used to search the internet for sounds that can then be saved as ringtones, notifications, or alarms.

Shazam [free] allows Android device users to identify the music playing around them, as well as discover song lyrics, and other music related information and tracks.

iOS

Shazam [free] allows iOS device users to identify the music playing around them, as well as discover song lyrics, and other music related information and tracks.

Computer – n/a

Web

300 Monks [free] provides a comprehensive source of royalty free music.

ccMixter [free] is a free music site that is community based and promotes a remix culture. *A cappella* and remix tracks licensed under Creative Commons are available for download and use in creative works.

FMA (Free Music Archive) [free] provides access to a range of free music based on a wide variety of genre. The music is offered free under various licenses for use.

Find Sounds [free] is a long-running service that can be used to search the internet for various sounds that can then be incorporated into various projects.

FreePlay Music [free] is a service that searches the internet for free music that can be used in YouTube videos and other projects.

Podcasting

Android

Podomatic Podcast & Mix Player [free] provides access to a wide variety of podcasts, listening in offline mode, and features such as a dynamic social feed so you can see the podcasts Facebook friends follow and like.

iOS

PodOmatic Podcast Player [free] provides access to a wide variety of podcasts, listening in offline mode, and features such as a dynamic social feed so you can see the podcasts Facebook friends follow and like.

Computer

Audacity [free] is a free multi-track audio recorder and editor with some very powerful features that include those for adding effects to files and conducting analysis of the audio recorded.

iTunes [free] offers media on demand and a way to organize and enjoy music, movies, and TV shows, as well as accessing and subscribing to podcasts and screencasts.

LoudBlog [free] is a Content Management System (CMS) for podcasts. This program automatically generates skinnable websites and RSS-feeds for audio and video podcasts, including provision for show notes and links.

PodcastGenerator [free] is an open source content management system for podcast publishing. It provides a comprehensive range of tools to manage all aspects of podcast publishing.

PodProducer [free] allows for the recording of voice and the adding of effects.

Web

ESLPod [free] provides a range of podcast content tailored to second-language learners of English from specific topics through to test-taking guides.

FeedForAll [free] allows for the creation, editing, and publishing of RSS feeds.

Feedity [free] is an online tool for creating an RSS feed for any web page, with an option to upgrade to a premium account that offers additional features.

FETCHRSS: RSS Generator [free] is an online RSS feed generator, that can create a feed out of almost any web page, automatically updates the RSS feed when new content is added to the web page, and generates an RSS for a social networking site.

OPML Viewer [free] allows users to view the contents of outline processor markup language (OPML) files.

Podcast Alley [free] is the place to go if you are interested in podcasts, want to gain access to the top podcasts, and want to find out the latest news about podcasts.

Pod Gallery [free] is a podcasting website where podcasters can share their episodes, and where listeners can subscribe.

QT-ESL Podcasts [free] provides a range of podcasts that cover oral grammar practice and includes scripts and worksheets.

SoundCloud [free] is a social sound platform where anyone is able to create and share audio.

Podcatchers

Android

Podcast Player [free] provides a range of podcast discovery options and tools, along with a range of features including a sleep timer, video support, intelligent silence skip and volume boost, as well as support for tablet, Chromecast, and Android Wear.

Podcast Republic [free] is an application that is ad-supported. It offers a variety of features from podcast discovery and automatic downloading through to storage management, sleep timer, and car mode. Support is also included from Chromecast and Android Wear.

Pocket Casts [paid] shows subscribed podcasts in a tile format, with easy sorting and categorization functions. Video podcast is also supported, along with auto-download and cleanup of downloaded and played episodes to save on storage space. Several features allow it to stand out, including a sleep timer as well as its cross-platform nature that grants it the ability to sync between multiple devices and mobile operating systems.

iOS

Overcast: Podcast Player [free] provides a combination of powerful audio and podcast management features. The application comes with a wide variety of features that allow it to download episodes, send notifications of new episodes, and play content offline or by streaming. It can also normalize speech levels, and speed through gaps and silence in podcasts.

Castro: High Fidelty Podcasts [free] is a simple and easy to use podcatcher. It provides a simple design with automatic episode download, dynamic storage management, along with episode streaming.

Pocket Casts [paid] shows subscribed podcasts in a tile format, with easy sorting and categorization functions. Video podcast is also supported, along with auto-download and cleanup of downloaded and played episodes to save on storage space. Several features allow it to stand out, including a sleep timer as well as its cross-platform nature that grants it the ability to sync between multiple devices and mobile operating systems.

Computer

gPodder [free] is an open source media aggregator and podcast client. It is able to store information in the cloud on which shows you have listened to, and it allows for the local installation of the client for download of content.

iTunes [free] is a comprehensive media aggregator that provides comprehensive support for media management, the audio and video playback of local media, podcast search and subscription, along with automatic downloads, syncing and streaming, and many other features.

Juice [free] is a long-standing cross platform no-frills podcast aggregator that is open source, and specifically designed to manage podcasts. Features include auto cleanup, centralized feed management, and for Windows users, accessibility options for the blind and visually impaired.

Web

Cloud Caster [free] is a web-based podcaster which works across all mobile devices. It syncs progress and playlists across platforms, and provides search and support for audio and video podcasts.

Presentations

Android

Glogster [free] allows students using an Android-based device to create online multimedia posters, or Glogs, from a combination of media types (from audio, graphic, to video), and hyperlinks.

Google Slides [free] allows Android device users with a Google account a means of creating, editing, and collaborating with others on presentations.

LinkedIn SlideShare [free] allows Android device users the ability to search and explore for a variety of presentations, infographics, and documents on topics of their interest.

Microsoft PowerPoint [free] allows users to view PowerPoint presentations on their device for free, and to make edits and changes on the go.

iOS

Glogster [free] allows students using an iOS device to create online multimedia posters, or Glogs, from a combination of media types (from audio, graphic, to video), and hyperlinks.

Google Slides [free] allows iOS device users with a Google account a means of creating, editing, and collaborating with others on presentations.

Keynote [free] is a powerful presentation app that allows users to develop comprehensive presentations with animations, transitions, and multimedia elements.

LinkedIn SlideShare [free] allows iOS device users the ability to search and explore for a variety of presentations, infographics, and documents on topics of their interest.

Microsoft PowerPoint [free] allows users to view PowerPoint presentations on their device for free, and to make edits and changes on the go.

Computer

Microsoft PowerPoint [paid] is a comprehensive presentation software application, and is perhaps the most used and recognizable.

Keynote [free] is a powerful presentation app that allows users to develop comprehensive presentations with animations, transitions, and multimedia elements.

Web

Bunkr [free] is a presentation tool that displays any online content including social media posts, images, videos, audio, articles, and files.

Glogster [free] allows students to create online multimedia posters, or Glogs, from a combination of media types (from audio, graphic, to video), and hyperlinks.

Google Slides [free] allows those with a Google account, a means of creating, editing, and collaborating with others on presentations.

LinkedIn SlideShare [free] allows users to search for presentations, infographics, documents and other items on topics of their interest.

Microsoft PowerPoint Online [free] extends the Microsoft PowerPoint experience to the web browser with OneDrive integration, and allows users to create, edit, and view files on the go.

Prezi [free] is a visually oriented presentation packaged that also allows users to upload PowerPoint slides, and customize them, or use a variety of their own images, text, audio, and video.

Slidebean [free] offers a one-click presentation development system that incorporates a variety of templates into the design of presentations.

Slides [free] is a place for creating, presenting, and sharing slide decks.

Swipe [free] allows users to share a presentation link with anyone across any device, and it allows viewers to interact with the presentation on several levels, from collaboration through to taking polls.

VoiceThread [free] allows users to import various media such as images, PowerPoints, and PDFs. It provides a means of making audio or video recordings concerning those media artifacts, and it also allows other users to reply to the initial comments, by audio or video means, as the presentation progresses.

Publishing

Android

Book Creator Free [free] offers a simple means of creating a variety of ebooks including picture books, comic and photo books, and journals and textbooks. It allows for the use of images, narration, texts, annotations and drawings.

Book Writer Free [free] is a simple book creation application that allows users to share their content with others.

My Story Builder [free] is a simple, 'suitable for children', book editor.

Scribble: Kids Book Maker [paid] is an application that allows children to write, illustrate, and publish their own comprehensive stories in a range of formations including video export. It contains a series of story starters, stickers, and backgrounds to help them work on creating stories from the start.

iOS

> *Book Creator Free* [free] offers a simple means of creating a variety of ebooks including picture books, comic and photo books, and journals and textbooks. It allows for the use of images, narration, texts, annotations and drawings.

> *Creative Book Builder* [paid] is a professional ebook editor and generator which can also extend the utility of ebooks through the use of a range of widgets.

> *Demibooks Composer Pro* [free] builds interactive books with animation, audio, images, and effects.

> *Scribble Press – Creative Book Maker for Kids* [paid] contains a series of story starters, stickers and backgrounds to help get young kids working on creating stories that can be turned into ebooks.

Computer

> *Android Book App Maker* [paid] provides users with the ability to turn content into a flip-book app.

> *iBooks* Author [free] provides a series of templates and styles to assist in the development of ebooks for the iBook store.

Kotobee [free] provides free software to assist in the creation of ebooks and libraries for a range of platforms.

Web

Blurb [paid] is just one of many online services that can assist in the creation of ebooks.

QR Codes

Android

I-nigma QR & Barcode Scanner (free) is a versatile barcode and QR code reader that can scan a multitude of codes and share these codes as well.

QR Code Reader (free) is a simple QR Code and product barcode scanner.

QR Droid Code Scanner (free) is a powerful barcode, QR code, and Data Matrix scanner that offers multi-language support.

iOS

Bakodo – Barcode Scanner and QR Barcode Reader (free) scans all types of QR codes and barcodes.

QR Reader for iPhone (free) scans a variety of codes including QR codes and barcodes, and features auto-detect scanning.

QRafter – QR Code and Barcode Reader and Generator (free) is a two-dimensional barcode scanner for iOS. Along with a variety of useful features, it can scan and generate QR codes.

Computer

CodeTwo QR Code Desktop Reader (free) allows users to scan QR codes directly from their screen onto their desktop. Users select the QR code to be read by selecting the area with a QR code using their mouse.

QR-Code Studio (free) is for Mac and Windows computers. The QR code maker software is freeware.

Web

QR Code Generator (free) creates QR codes, in a limited number of formats, for free.

QR Stuff QR Code Generator (free) creates QR codes from a various types of data such as website URLs, image files, PDF files, and so on, with static and dynamic embedding options.

The QR Code Generator (free) allows for the free scan and generation of QR codes for a variety of uses.

Rubrics

Android

> *Daily Rubric: Any Curriculum* [free] allows teachers to create and use rubrics from their Android device. Rubrics can be designed from curriculum outcomes, or based on the pre-loaded Common Core Standards.

iOS

> *Easy Assessment* [paid] offers a means to capture and assess performance based on custom created rubrics, scale, or criteria.

> *Rubrics* [paid] allows instructors to track student performance and produce reports based on custom rubrics and grading options.

Computer – n/a

Web

> *Kathy Shrock's Guide to Everything: Assessment and Rubrics* [free] provides access to a wide range of rubrics to help guide assessment of students.

> *iRubric* [free] is a website where instructors can create their own rubrics, or they can build off those made available from other instructors.

RubiStar [free] allows instructors to create their own rubrics using templates designed for core subjects as well as art, music, and multimedia.

Screencasting

Android

AZ Screen Recorder [free] is a screen recording application that offers several features, including the ability to capture the front camera as well as screen recording. It also provides video trimming.

ilos Screen Recorder [free] is a simple application that records the screen and provides audio capture as well.

Telecine [free] is an open source application that allows screen recording through the use of overlays.

iOS

Doceri [trial/paid] combines screencasting, desktop control, and an interactive whiteboard in one application, with control through Airplay or through Mac or PC.

Educreations Interactive Whiteboard [free] is an interactive whiteboard and screencasting tool that allows annotation, animation, and narration of a number of content types.

Screenchomp [free] allows users to annotate pictures or to use the application as a whiteboard. Any work completed with the application can be saved automatically to the internet.

Computer

ilos screen recorder [free] automatically uploads content to their servers for storage and playback.

Screencast-O-Matic [free] offers fifteen minutes of recording time for free, both for screen and webcam, and allows users to save to places such as YouTube or as a video file.

TechSmith Camtasia Studio [free trial] is a comprehensive screen recording application that allows for audio and webcam capture as well as highlighting, adding media, and editing of recordings.

Web – n/a

Storyboarding and Scripting

Android

Ray Story Board [free] is a simple storyboard creator that lets users build storyboards from photos or gallery images, create multiple storyboards, and animate them using a slideshow feature.

Storyboard Studio [paid] is a mobile storyboarding writing tool that is suitable for artists and non-artists alike.

iOS

Penultimate [free] provides a natural feel of writing and sketching on paper, and connects to Evernote.

Storyboard Composer [paid] is a mobile storyboard previsualiztion composer for animators, art directors, film students, film directors, or anyone who would like to visualize their story.

Computer

FrameForge Previz Studio [paid] allows users to develop and previsualize films, TV shows, commercials, or similar projects at a professional level.

Storyboardpro [paid] is professional level software that combines drawing and animation tools with camera controls.

StoryBoard Quick Studio [paid] allows for the fast creation of storyboards with QuickShots, has a print-to-sketch feature, and comes with a series of character poses for integration into storylines.

Web

Google Docs [free] can be used, along with any note-taking or document editor, as a make-shift storyboard by integrating photos or pictures into the document to outline a process or the actions for a story. It is also available as an Android and iOS app.

StoryboardThat [free trial] offers an edition that allows educators to build diagrams, and visualize workflow. It features a drag and drop interface and an extensive image library.

Story Creation Apps

Android

StoryMaker 1 [free] provides a means of creating stories using templates and overlays, and the possibility of using audio, photos, or video.

Storehouse [free] allows users to share a collection of photos in a collage or album, or by telling a story that links the photos.

iOS

StoryKit [free] allows for the creation of an electronic storybook through the use of images, simple drawings, recording of sound, and by the addition of text.

Storyrobe [paid] makes photo-based slideshows with voice recording.

FotoBabble [free] adds audio to a photo to make a talking postcard.

Sock Puppets [free] lets users create lip-synced videos with characters. Various puppets, props, scenery, and backgrounds can be used.

Computer

Cartoon Story Maker 1.1 [free] is a simple program that creates 2D cartoon stories with conversations, dialogs (recorded and/or speech bubble), and various backgrounds.

StoryMaker [free/trial] is game-based software that asks for parts of speech (such as nouns, verbs, adjectives), and these are then inserted into a story with sometimes comical results. Educators can edit and customize aspects of the aspects of the program for their context. Backgrounds can be imported, but character templates are built in.

Web

Littlebirdtales [free] provides younger learners the ability to create digital storybooks.

Pixton [free/paid] is a visual writing tool that allows users to make a comic using images, clipart backgrounds and artwork, as well as speech bubbles.

Storynet.org [free] is a website that aims at connecting people to and through storytelling.

StoryJumper [free] allows users to create illustrated storybooks from scratch or from existing templates.

Video Editing

Android

VideoShow – Video Editor [free] is an all-in-one video editor and slideshow producer that provides music, themes, filters, emojis, as well as text input.

VidTrim [free] is a video editor and organizer that allows the trimming, editing, and saving of videos.

VivaVideo: Free Video Editor [free] is a comprehensive video editor and movie maker that facilitates the creation of video-based stories.

WeVideo [free] is a comprehensive and easy to use video editor that can mix images, text, video, and audio.

iOS

iMovie [paid] is video creation and editing software that can create easily shareable content.

Splice [free] is a video editor that adds music and effects to images and videos with narration. It includes access to free songs, sound effects, text overlays, transitions, filters, and various editing tools.

ReelDirector II [paid] is a full-featured video editing app.

WeVideo [free] is an easy to use and comprehensive video editor that can mix audio, images, text, and audio.

Computer

Windows Movie Maker [free] is a video editing software application that allows for narration, audio, images, and video to be mixed and edited with transitions and special effects.

Web

Video Toolbox [free] is an online video editing and conversion tool.

WeVideo [free] is a comprehensive and easy to use web-based video editor that can mix images, text, video, and audio together to form a compelling story.

Video Resources

Android

> *TED* [free] provides more than 2,000 TED talks from various people by topic and mood, and on a variety of topics.

> *Vimeo* [free] is a variety of videos are available across a wide variety of topics and genres, with users having the ability to upload their own content as well.

> *YouTube* [free] allows for editing and uploading of videos, where one can subscribe to various channels that offer a wide variety of videos on various topics and genres.

iOS

> *TED* [free] provides more than 2,000 TED talks from various people by topic and mood, and on a variety of topics.

> *Vimeo* [free] provides a variety of videos which are available across a wide variety of topics and genres. Users are able to upload their own content as well.

YouTube [free] allows for editing and uploading of videos, where once can subscribe to various channels that offer a wide variety of videos on various topics and genres.

Computer – n/a

Web

Clipcanvas [free] allows for the download of 600,000 royalty free HD and 4K video and film clips.

Mazwai [free] maintains a collection of free to use HD video clips and footage, and some unique time-lapse and slow motion video footages that are provided under the Creative Commons Attribution license if used commercially.

Motion Backgrounds for Free [free] is a place to download professional quality motion backgrounds and video footage.

Motion Elements [free] is a good source for premium stock videos, offering around 400 videos for free, as well as free After Effects templates.

Neo's Clip Archive [free] offers nearly 3,500 free video clips sorted by 25 categories free for use for personal, non-commercial purposes.

Pexels Videos [free] brings under one roof a video library of Creative Commons Zero licensed stock videos from a variety of different sources.

SaveTube [free] allows users to rip YouTube videos to their local computer in various audio or video-based formats.

Savevideo.me [free] allows users to rip videos from a variety of sites to their local computer.

TeacherTube [free] is an online resource that helps users to view and share videos, photos, audio, and documents on almost any topic.

WebQuests

Android – n/a

iOS – n/a

Computer – n/a

Web

Building a WebQuest [free] is a comprehensive overview of the template to follow when there is a need to construct a WebQuest.

Having Fun with Reading [free] is a WebQuest for college and adult level learners of English, where learners interact with texts and complete activities that promote cooperative and collaborative learning along with reading narrative comprehension skills.

Idioms in Your Pocket [free] is a WebQuest that is designed for high school and adult ESL students, and it allows them to discover the various meanings of English idioms.

OneStopEnglish WebQuests [free] provides a selection of WebQuests covering major holidays.

Pre-Writing Your WebQuest [free] provides prompts for users to complete in order to develop a WebQuest.

QuestGarden [free/paid] is a site designed by Bernie Dodge, the creator of WebQuests, for use by pre- and in-service teachers, professional developers, other educators, and those who work with them. The site provides hosting and template creation of WebQuests that then become searchable.

Using WebQuests to Teach English [free] is a WebQuest that can be used to teach teachers about WebQuests.

WebQuestDirect [free] is described as the world's largest searchable directory of WebQuest reviews.

WebQuest.Org [free] provides comprehensive information pertaining to the WebQuest model, and is run by Bernie Dodge, the creator of WebQuests.

Zunal [free/paid] is a site for educators to create, host, and then share their WebQuests with others.

Wikis

Android

EveryWiki: Wikipedia++ [free] aims to provide access to many wikis from a central application.

wikiHow [free] is the application associated with the leading how-to-guide wikiHow. It allows for searching of the wiki to find step-by-step instructions on how to complete almost any task.

iOS

Hack My Life – Life Hack Wiki [free] is an application that seeks to provide access to all possible life hacks. A life hack is a strategy or technique that can be used or adopted to allow for better time management or for getting more out of everyday activities.

Lyrically [free] offers access to a list of song lyrics curated by fans. Searches can be undertaken by track, artist, or by song, and there is support for in-app purchases.

Computer

DokuWiki [free] is a PHP based highly customizable and fully extensible wiki software platform. The advantage is that it requires no databases as all the data is stored in plain text, and for this reason, it is very popular and used by many sites. It has a variety of useful features, from locking to avoid edits through to a spam blacklist.

MediaWiki [free] is open-source and it is the wiki software used by Wikipedia. It is available in a number of languages, released under a general public license (GPL), and written in PHP: Hypertext Preprocessor (PHP) a server-side scripting language. There are many extensions and plugins available for free, including a what-you-see-is-what-you-get (WYSIWYG) editor.

Web

PBworks [free] (formerly PBwiki) is a real-time collaborative editing system with several solutions including one for educators. It offers a single workspace, where student accounts can be created without email addresses, and easy editing without the need for coding.

PmWiki [free] is a wiki tool that gives user-access control over individual pages, so they can be set for access by specific people with it being possible to set different passwords for each page. The software also allows for navigation trails through individual sections, insertion of tables, and provides a printable layout.

Wikidot [free] offers members the ability to create a wiki-based website with forums, where they can create a community, or publish and share documents and content.

Wikispaces [free] is a wiki hosting service that provides educators with a means to monitor student progress in real time and the ability to easily create projects and assign them to students, as well as editing tools and a social newsfeed.

Teacher Notes

Android

iOS

Computer

_____

_____

_____

_____

_____

_____

_____

_____

_____

_____

_____

_____

_____

_____

_____

_____

_____

_____

_____

_____

Web

_____

_____

_____

_____

_____

_____

_____

_____

_____

_____

_____

_____

_____

_____

_____

_____

_____

_____

_____

_____

_____

_____

16
References

Ali, A. D. (2016). Effectiveness of Using Screencast Feedback on EFL Students' Writing and Perception. *English Language Teaching, 9*(8), 106-121.

Assink, M. (2006). Inhibitors of disruptive innovation capability: A conceptual model. *European Journal of Innovation Management, 9*(2), 215-233.

Bell, T., Cockburn, A., Wingkvist, A., & Green, R. (2007). Podcasts as a Supplement in Tertiary Education: An Experiment with Two Computer Science Courses. *Conference on Mobile Learning Technologies and Applications.* February 19, Auckland, New Zealand.

Christenson, C. M., & Raynor, M. E. (2003). *The innovator's solution: Creating and sustaining Successful Growth.* Cambridge, MA: Harvard University Press.

Davis, A., & McGrail, E. (2009). 'Proof-revising' with Podcasting: Keeping Readers in Mind as Students Listen to and Rethink their Writing. *Reading Teacher 62*(6), 522-529.

Hadjioannour, X., & Hutchinson, M. (2014). Fostering Awareness through Transmediation: Preparing Pre-Service Teachers for Critical Engagement with Multicultural Literature. *International Journal of Multicultural Education, 16*(1), 1-20.

Hammersley, B. (2004, February 12). Audible Revolution. *The Guardian*. Retrieved from https://www.theguardian.com/media/2004/feb/12/broadcasting.digitalmedia

Holec, H. (1987). The Learner as Manager: Managing Learning or Managing to learn? In A. Enden, & J. Rubin (Eds.), *Learner Strategies in Language Learning* (pp. 145-156). London: Prentice Hall.

Liou, H. C., & Peng, S. Y. (2009). Training Effects on Computer-Mediated Peer Review. *System 37*(3), 514-525.

Mayer, R. E. (2003). The Promise of Multimedia Learning: Using the Same Instructional Design Methods across Different Media. *Learning and Instruction, 13*(2), 125.

Sampson, D., Karagiannidis, C., Schenone, A., Cardinali, F. (2002). Knowledge-on-demand in e-Learning and e-working Settings. *Educational Technology & Society*, 5(2).

Udell, J. (2004, November, 15). Name that Genre. *InfoWorld*. Retrieved from http://jonudell.net/udell/2004-11-15-name-that-genre.html

About the Book

In a world where content is increasingly required for just-in-time learning, and knowledge is essentially needed only on demand, podcasting and screencasting find themselves extremely conducive for learning. They also offer innovative and creative ways of providing education to students, with episodic use and production allowing for the development of a broad range of essential life skills as well as the practice of key second-language skills. This is particularly poignant for the teaching of English to speakers of other languages (TESOL) as a means of meeting the immediate needs of students through such models as targeted instruction, flipping of the classroom, and formative assessment. The pedagogical possibilities offered by podcasting and screencasting are included, along with the steps involved in planning, producing, and publishing them. Following this is an overview of instructional strategies, tutorials, photocopiable handouts and templates, evaluation techniques, and a comprehensive list of a wide variety of resources.

About the Author

David Kent is an Assistant Professor at the Graduate School of TESOL-MALL at Woosong University in the Republic of Korea. He has been working and teaching in Korea since 1995, and with a Doctorate of Education from Curtin University in Australia, he is a specialist in computer assisted language learning (CALL) and the teaching of English to speakers of other languages (TESOL). He has presented at international conferences, as well as published a number of peer-reviewed journal articles, books, and book chapters in his areas of specialization.

Also by David Kent

A Loanword Approach to the Teaching of
English as a Foreign Language in Korea:
Exploring the Effectiveness of a Multimedia Curriculum

Teaching with Technology:
Integrating Technology into the TESOL Classroom

TESOL Strategy Guides
Digital Storytelling
The Prezi Presentation Paradigm
Podcasts and Screencasts